You Have the Nerve to Call Yourself a Roman Catholic!

I

RDR PUBLISHING LLC *Read Dream Rejoice .....*

You Have the Nerve to Call Yourself a Roman Catholic!

Author:

Raymond D. Reifinger III

Copyright

RDR PUBLISHING LLC *Read Dream Rejoice .....*

P. O. Box 441
Bethlehem, Pa. 18016-0441
Web Site: www.RDRPublishing.com
E-Mail: info@RDRPublishing.com

Lulu Distributing
Raleigh, London, Toronto and Bangalore

ISBN 978-0-9827250-1-6

ISBN 978-0-9827250-1-6
Copyright 2010 © by Raymond D. Reifinger III

Printed in the United States of America
First Edition

Statistics
Words: 54,942
Lines: 7,156
Pages: 224

Dedication

To my mother and father, Elizabeth and Raymond Reifinger Junior. May they rest in peace. The greatest human parents a child could be blessed with. I dedicate this book in honor of their loving care and excellent work in raising us children. This book could not have been written without their wonderful guidance in providing an excellent foundation for me to build upon in concert with love, respect and morals through the Roman Catholic faith. Thank you.....

Introduction

I would like to be able to say this is my fifteenth book and I'm the author of your dreams. In reality, I must humbly say this is my first book. I also have to say you may not want to hear everything said in this book, but you should read it anyway. This book is directed towards Roman Catholics, but may be read by anyone. In fact, I would prefer that it is read by everyone to aid in getting my message out to as many people as humanly possible. If it doesn't apply to you, I would appreciate it if you could give the book to someone you might know who could benefit from it.

I'm, very possibly, just the guy sitting next you in Church. I feel I have been inspired by the Lord above to write this book and to get this message out to everyone, especially Roman Catholics, who through my belief are held to a higher standard. I have had this burning in my heart to do this, which is why I feel I have been called by the Lord, for probably about eight years now and have been working on this book off and on ever since. Now that I have the opportunity of putting this book in print I hope I don't drop the ball and everyone can get some value from it. The message is extremely important and I hope to do it justice.

I have no aspiration in professing any political views, getting anyone upset, mad, chastising or hurting anyone. My intent is not to achieve fame or great wealth. What is written comes from the heart for the glory of God, Him alone. If it should happen, you are dissatisfied with the book for any reason it may be comforting for you to know that over half of any profits made will be going directly to the Roman Catholic Church.

Many people have asked me why I'm a Roman

Catholic. First of all, I'm a cradle Catholic, born into the Roman Catholic religion through my parents. However, this is not my reason. My answer is simple, direct and to the point. I tell them to "read" the bible. You can see, in the holy bible itself, and read where our Lord Jesus Christ himself started the Roman Catholic religion and named our first Pope in the great gospel of Matthew. Who better to follow, than our Lord Jesus, the son of God himself? Why anyone would look elsewhere is beyond me. It doesn't have to be anymore difficult than that.

Matthew 16: 15-19

He said to them, "But who do you say that I am?"
Simon Peter said in reply, "You are the Messiah, the
son of the living God." Jesus said to him in reply,
"Blessed are you Simon son of Jonah. For flesh and
blood has not revealed this to you, but my heavenly
Father, And so I say to you, you are Peter, and upon this
rock I will build my church and the gates of the
netherworld shall not prevail against it. I will give you
the keys to the kingdom of heaven. Whatever you bind
on earth shall be bound in heaven; and whatever you
shall loose on earth shall be loosed in heaven."

Right from the Lord Jesus himself! Appointing Saint Peter as the first Pope of the Roman Catholic Church. Giving him the keys to heaven and putting him in charge of guiding the Church along the path of light and truthfulness defined by our Lord. Why should you need to go elsewhere? The objective of the Church is to get all of us to heaven and what better to follow than the Church of the Lord Jesus! The Roman Catholic Church.

You will notice my reference list is quite short. The

reason is the biggest percentage of what I will say comes right straight from the heart and from the bible. From a layman, not a priest or a theologian, from the guy most possibly sitting next to you in Church. I pray and hope most people in Church feel the same as I do. There is too much silence, we need to say out loud and everywhere what we are thinking and to make known our feelings on the atrocity in this country of abortion. What we need to do is to break the silence and save our unborn babies. To predispose others to do the same before it is too late, before another child succumbs to the ugly and deplorable fate of abortion or as I prefer to call it, **murder**.

The goal in writing this book is to defend and hopefully save the lives of the unborn babies of this nation, of this world. If this book helps to rescue even just one baby from the fate of abortion, it will be a success and priceless in my eyes and worth any and all the efforts in producing it. Of course, I aspire, with your help, to save "all" the unborn infants in this world from such a destiny and to end this despicable act all together.

I sincerely hope you enjoy the book and possibly gain some insight into what abortion really is, at least in laymen's terms and why it must be stopped. I intend to say some of the things, which never seem to get said, but should. Some of my statements are rather bold and should or need to be, to emphasize their importance, not to cause injury or to be an assault on any one person and I name no names. I know there are plenty of very good Roman Catholics out there who are doing excellent work in the service of our Lord and obviously my statements would not apply to those of such stature. I'm more concerned with our brothers and sisters who seem to be going down the wrong path and ignoring or treating with deference even some of the basics of our religion.

It appears abortion these days is treated in a very insouciant way or as just another alternative or option in life. My hope is to explain how a decision like this is a very pernicious act spiritually to your soul and obviously a deadly act to the unborn child.

Please begin reading this book with an open mind and heart. Open your eyes, so you might see and open your ears, so you might hear. My intent is not to hurt, but to save lives. Remember, this is just the guy sitting next to you in your Church, not a famous author or a degree possessing theologian, just someone, no one in particular, a person just like you speaking directly from the heart.

I can't compel you to feel any particular way. I can only express why I feel the way I do and hope to convey to you the importance the decision of abortion is and why you should take care in making that decision both for yours and your baby's live's and souls. If successful, I will help you to understand why there is only really one "correct" judgment to make. Please ask yourself, "What would Jesus do?" If you do that, then dedicate yourself to some serious contemplation on the matter. I'm confident you will consummate with the appropriate decision.

There are two sets of laws, there is man's law and there is God's law. My aim is simply to express the importance of God's law over man's and your duty as a Christian or as any person desiring to do what is right and to avoid any acts of moral turpitude in our society today. When there is a conflict between man's law and God's law it should register with you something is wrong. The red flag should pop up. Something needs to be changed and I will give you a hint, it isn't God's law. God's law should be your standard, a yardstick from which everything else is measured, a place where you can truthfully discern the differences between right and wrongful acts, good and evil. I will attempt to delve deeper into that and more as you read on.

If you should happen to know someone battling the decision of abortion in their lives please give them a copy of this book. Hopefully it will help them in making a moral and spiritually correct decision, when it comes to abortion and realize there is really only one decision to make and that would be to accept the gift God has given them with great joy and happiness. You just may save the life of an unborn child yourself.

Sincerely,

Raymond D. Reifinger III
Jan., 09, 2010

Acknowledgments

Inspired By Jesus's Teachings
....Spiritual

Kimberly T. Schmid
....Consultant

RDR PUBLISHING LLC

Read Dream Rejoice .....

You Have the Nerve to Call Yourself a Roman Catholic!

Author:

Raymond D. Reifinger III

Contents

Part I
Abortion

Chapter 1

Legalized Murder
(Oops ..... I Mean Pro-Choice)!

How can we say, "One Nation, under God" and at the same time permit "pro-choice" to exist in our society, our country, the great United States of America? You really can't be serious, can you? How can you call "pro-choice," which is really a very nice way of sugar coating the horrible word abortion, anything other than **"LEGALIZED MURDER"**?

Have we no morals today? Are we going to just permit this heinous act to go on forever? Should we sit back and watch the moral decadence of our society pass through generation after generation from our recliners, while sipping our coffee, without lifting a finger? How can you stand it? I have had enough! I am totally spent. I can't take it anymore! I'M FED UP TO HERE! Let the records show I am holding my hand atop my head! This has got to come

- - - - - - - - - - - - - - -

to an end and the sooner the better.

Do we think the problem is going to go away by itself? This country is full, to the top, with the amoral and the immoral. I think I know why. It is because we are sitting in our recliners, while sipping our coffee, doing absolutely nothing. If you do nothing, nothing happens.

I hear this question posed all the time. "What is the biggest problem in America Today?" It isn't the economy, it isn't health care, it isn't Wall Street, it isn't free speech, its **"Legalized Murder"**! Complete apathy for the rights of our future citizens, our unborn babies. Don't our babies have rights? We are totally missing the boat here. Where are our priorities? Sometimes I wish I was having a nightmare and eventually I will wake up and everything will be all right and there will be no more senseless killing of our unborn babies. If you don't appreciate the sanctity of life, everything else goes out the door. The sanctity of life should form the foundation from which everything else sprouts from. If you don't have respect for the life of one human being, you don't have respect for any human being. We are supposed to be a civilized nation!

When I was still in school, somewhere about the fourth or fifth grade, we were having a discussion about China. The teacher said they had a dictator over there and one of the students asked, "What is the difference between us and the people there?" The teacher said, "We have freedom here, over there if you don't do what you are told they either put you in jail or they kill you. They have no regard for human life, human life is not sacred there as it is here. They don't think of people as we do. To them a person's life doesn't mean much, if anything, but here we value

You Have the Nerve to Call Yourself a Roman Catholic!
Chapter 1 Page 20

everyone's life very much." Are we becoming another country like China? Do we still have respect for the sanctity of human life? It appears it is getting tougher to tell the difference.

I'm sorry. I'm trying to be as humane as I can possibly be. I am also disgusted, thoroughly and utterly disgusted and you should be too. We are talking about a human life here, in fact literally millions of human lives. We are talking about an abomination to the Lord! You can't hide this from the Lord. He sees and hears all.

I know we are supposed to be tip-toeing around and whispering these kinds of things and I know why. Why, because this is a horrific and hideous display of injustice to mankind, a disgrace to our nation, a disgrace to the Lord. Oh, and above all, it **"embarrasses"** people! Oh, we can't have that. We don't want to get the people involved upset. I wonder if the unborn baby gets upset? They are ashamed and they should be, so they don't want anything to be heard or even mentioned on the topic. You know what I'm talking about and as that is the case, then it should stand to reason people even considering these heinous acts know in their hearts they are doing wrong. The holocaust of the Jews was horrible to the max and I don't want to detract from the atrocity on human lives it claimed, but abortion right here in the United States has claimed even more lives. This is a war people and it is claiming millions of lives of the innocent, the tiniest, our defenseless, our unborn babies! Where are the human rights activists?

I heard one of the great leaders of this sovereign nation, when asked if he would approve of his children getting an abortion, he actually said it would be all right if the pregnancy was unplanned, because he couldn't see a lifetime of "burden" being placed on them. He even approves of "infanticide"! A **"BURDEN"**, this must make **abortion**, **legalized murder**, okay right? This is what we call our gift from God, a miracle in the making, this is merely just a "burden"? Then, I repeat, we say this is "One Nation, under God".

You have the nerve to call yourself a Roman Catholic!

You allow this, these atrocities, to take place in your very own country right under your nose and you do nothing? You have the audacity to help elect someone like this to public office! We, Roman Catholics, are supposed to be the models for the remainder of society to look to and imitate. We are held to a higher degree or standard. We are supposed to show others the straight path, the path of light and truthfulness! Bow your heads in shame and ask the Lord for forgiveness, for if you have done nothing, you have sinned!

Shame on you! **Shame** on you!

It doesn't matter if you're a Democrat, Republican, Independent or whatever. The politics should not be the problem, it's our morality. We could make politics the problem, but it shouldn't even be involved. Politics are one thing, the lives of the citizens of this wonderful country another. Everyone should be concerned, regardless of their politics, about the welfare and lives of "all" their people, even the ones not yet born and especially these ones who are most in need of our care, the most defenseless, the most fragile, our innocent little babies.

Every day, every second of every day, there are miracles being made by our Lord. You are a miracle, I'm a miracle, everyone you look at is a miracle of life sacred to each other and to our Lord. Do you really want to destroy the work of our creator? Don't you feel your life is sacred? I hope you would answer yes. Don't you think everyone thinks their own life is sacred? Of course they do!

Every life is a novel in itself, authored by our Lord. Every day you live another page written by the Lord bringing you adventure and taking you on a journey of the unknown. You never know what the next day will bring, what is around the next corner. Sometimes you can predict what is coming, sometimes not. But you never "really" know for sure what to expect. The really amazing thing is the Lord, who is authoring the novels of billions of people every day. Some very short, some not so short and some very long, yes the Lord even decides how long your novel will be and he doesn't let you know when the last page is going to be written. The last page is important and the Lord will decide when that should be.

Do you think our Lord wants you to put an abrupt end to your novel or the novel of anyone else? Do you think this is his plan? Myself, I believe everyone's novel if you could go in and read every last page would be exciting!

Legalized Murder (Oops ..... I Mean Pro-Choice)!

Knowing the details, all the secrets, all the trials and tribulations, the ups, the downs, everything, this particular creation of the Lord had to deal with and how that person managed the journey the Lord provided for him or her. You might say some people are boring, but I only think that is true because you don't know all the details, all the secrets. Some people tell all and some don't, but in the end I truly think everyone is amazing and every novel exciting and a wonderful gift from the Lord for everyone to participate in and enjoy.

What do you think is in the novel of the aborted baby? A very short novel? Not very exciting? All the pages torn out? Would you like for your novel to be the same as these babies? The amazing and exciting journey of this baby's life, provided by our Lord, stolen, taken away permanently. Is this justice? I know I wouldn't want my book to read the same. All my experiences, all that I have learned, all my memories, all my thoughts, all my ideas, all my friends, all my family, all my plans, all my good times, all my exciting times, all the beauty in the world my eyes have seen, all the wonderful music I have listened to, all the great food I have tasted, all the beautiful flowers, sunsets and sunrises I have seen, all my accomplishments, all the days I woke up and was still breathing, all taken away in one fell swoop. No, I'm thankful my novel is not that of an aborted baby. Talk about being cheated out of all the wonderful things in life forever! Never getting a chance to experience any of the great things in life. No, not every day is a great day, there are good days and bad days alike, but the bad days just help you to be more appreciative and that much more grateful for those good and great days. If you didn't have any bad days, you wouldn't really know just how good those good days are. Please sit back, relax and think about it, think real hard and long. All our lives are really unique and sacred and deserved to be lived to the fullest.

Now, I'm not without guilt myself, but no more. I can't just sit in the pew in Church every Sunday and remain silent anymore. Someone needs to speak up and let his or her voice be heard or this massacre of our unborn children will continue and continue and continue. We need to have respect for the sanctity of life, for our little miracles from heaven, they can't defend themselves. If we don't defend them, who will?

Every time I hear "pro-choice", which I really feel should be renamed "pro-murder", I want to gag, my stomach turns, I end up with a sick feeling all over. I really can't believe I have to say these things. They should be automatic, understood without a question. Have we forgotten about the fifth commandment? Do we remember any of the commandments? You can't be just half a Roman Catholic. You can't just say I like these commandments here, but I don't know about the rest of the commandments. You can't just stick your toe in the water, you must totally immerse yourself in the Roman Catholic faith. You must "live" our faith! Maybe we should do a review of at least the fifth commandment.

The Fifth Commandment, Exodus 20:13
"You shall not kill."

Right now I want you to look at everyone around you.

- - - - - - - - - - - - - -

Legalized Murder (Oops ..... I Mean Pro-Choice)!

Yes, go ahead and look! There is one thing everyone you have looked at and everyone in the world, for that matter, has in common. They "all" began as one cell at conception. You kill that "one" cell, you kill that person. They did not begin at birth! Birth is where you are introduced to the world, it isn't when your life began. It's black and white. No "sane" person can argue that point, period! If you do, you are rationalizing and you are going to rationalize yourself right straight to hell! You have to start growing from somewhere and that is from that single cell and onward. It doesn't take a doctor, scientist or some genius to figure that out. It is just plain common sense. One more thing. You will never be able to convince me there is a good reason for killing an unborn baby. Do you know why? None exists. There is no reason of any kind, **NONE!**

One of the arguments I hear a lot is in the first couple of months the single cell has not developed enough to be a complete person yet, so its okay to abort the pregnancy. Well, if you are going to make that presumption, the body isn't really fully developed until your about eighteen years of age. Why don't we extend the abortion window until lets say fifteen years of age? After all this child isn't fully developed yet. This will give us much more time to make our decision. Does this sound foolish? It should and so is that premise!

It is also said if you don't allow women to have abortions legally they will just go and get one by illegal means, maybe in a basement or in an unsanitary back room somewhere. My answer to that is simple. Take bank robbers for instance. You know if we put bank robbers in jail other people will rob banks and when those whom we put in jail get out of jail they will rob banks again, so why not make bank robbery legal. If you don't, they will just do it again when they get out or someone else will.

The arguments I hear for abortion are ridiculous, they make no sense if you do a little work investigating their theories. I can't stand it anymore, I feel I have to do something. Someone has to do something, say something, we can't just sit there! I can't go to Church every week, Sunday after Sunday and do nothing. I know there are people sitting next to me every week, who feel the same way. I can't help thinking what if I was one of those babies? What if you were one of those babies? What would we do? We would do nothing! We would be defenseless! Sit back in your chair for a moment and think about that. Think about it, real hard and long.

What do we do? We sit there loyally every Sunday in Church feeling all good about ourselves simply for being in attendance and then do nothing when we leave. The priests and nuns can't do it all, they need our help. They do what they can, but they can't do it all. Is this what our faith has taught us to do? I think not.

Every day goes by, every week, every month, every year and we do nothing. The biggest holocaust the world has ever known and we do nothing! We just bury our heads in the sand and ignore this slaughter of the most vulnerable of infants, our future citizens. We "do" whisper, because we don't want to offend anyone.

Do we care? Of course! However, we still do nothing. Well, I believe it is time something is done, the Lord is watching. The time is now! What are you going to tell the

- - - - - - - - - - - - - -

Legalized Murder (Oops ..... I Mean Pro-Choice)!

Lord on judgement day? Oops! Sorry! I was too busy with "my" life! I was going to, but I just didn't get the chance! I didn't want to "embarrass" anyone.

Wouldn't you want to be able to tell the Lord you did your best or even better, you succeeded in stopping this horrible slaughter of our babies? What could be better to have on your resume, on judgement day, than to say you helped put a stop to legalized murder in your country or even the world? I like the sound of that. Somehow, I think the Lord would like it too.

Do we value the principle of the sanctity of life? We most definitely do! If it is "our" life! I see every day on the television adds for all kinds of drugs, screening for diseases of all sorts, pills or operations to keep us alive even if it is for just one more day. We are exercising, pumping iron, jogging, dieting and doing anything and everything to extend our lives that much more. We have various creams, salves, lotions, emollients, oils and energy drinks to help make our bodies stay young just that much longer. Oh yes, we do appreciate the sanctity of "our" lives.

We will do any and everything to stay on this earth just one more day, week or year. I don't see anyone in a great hurry to leave the earth our heavenly Father provided for us. Oh we complain about it, but we are in no hurry to leave it. Maybe we should give our unborn babies a chance to do the same. I really think they would greatly appreciate the opportunity.

It's too bad we don't care for our "souls" as much as we care for our lives and bodies. We all would be saints! I am sure there are a few priests that would take my side on that one. What we really need to do is to put ourselves in the other person's shoes or at least "booties". I always try to do that when I'm making decisions involving other people. It usually gives you a real good perspective of the other person's plight. It tends to give you some really good insight on the situation at hand and maybe even give you the acumen to do the right thing. Many people don't skip a heart beat making the decision to abort their child. However, if you were to put yourself in that infant's booties, I am quite sure any decisions made would not be made as hastily.

We are talking about a person's life, people! I hear so often people say how they would do anything for their children, even give their lives. Hypocrites! "Except" for the tiniest of them, the most helpless, defenseless, powerless and the weakest of them. Talk is cheap and it can and has claimed many lives.

Keep in mind I feel I'm as guilty, at least at times, as anyone else. I'm not casting the first stone, by any means. I have sat in that Church too, doing nothing week after week. Well, with one exception, they, the unborn babies, are "always" in my daily prayers. However, I need to do more, you need to do more, we all need to do more, until the job gets done and our most precious little ones are at least in no danger of murder or even infanticide. I'm no saint, but I can't keep my mouth shut any longer. We kill in these great United States more infants in one year than all the people who lost their lives in all of our wars put together. This is just not right no matter how you cut it! Notice I said "we". If you're not part of the solution, you are part of the problem. I include myself in that statement and it gets me sick and that is exactly why I can't take it anymore. I have a conscience and I know you do too.

It makes us feel better when we say "pro-choice", oh certain words can give you such a good feeling inside. You are just allowing the mother to have her freedom of choice. What could be so bad about that? I heard Father John Corapi say, "Pro-choice, the choice has already been made!" In other words, if you are already pregnant, you made the choice. Has anyone ever heard of abstinence? If you don't know who Father John Corapi is, you should! He's one of the best proponents of the Roman Catholic faith I have ever heard. He makes you feel real good to be a Roman Catholic. It's not so much what he says, but how he says it. However, getting back to pro-choice, which sounds so much better than the word "abortion" or the word "MURDER". You know, the word murder is so crude, rough, rude and unrefined. Yes, it's much more pleasant to say pro choice, BUT NOT ANY DIFFERENT THAN SAYING MURDER!

I have heard and still hear the multitude of excuses. Everything from cosmetic reasons, yes, I said cosmetic reasons, to rape. "I want to get an abortion, because I don't want anyone to see me look fat". "I want to get an abortion, because I'm not ready to have a child yet and I won't be able to go out and have fun". "I'll have to stay home and watch the baby". "I don't have the money to raise a child". "I want to complete college first, I'll have another child later". "She's to immature to have this child now". "The father doesn't want to keep the baby". You know, all these really, really good reasons to have an abortion. To kill a little unborn child! Do you think I'm joking? These supposedly are good reasons to have an abortion. There are dozens more just like them! I'm sure you have heard many, just as bad, yourself. I could say a lot more, but I don't want to waste your time with such gibberish. If you're like me, I think they really look silly in print. Like, are you kidding me?

Now, rape is a tough one. No rational person would envy anyone who is the victim of rape or want to be in their shoes, but is it going to help anything by aborting the innocent product of the rape, the unborn child? The rapist commits a felony of rape and the victim commits what should be a felony, of murder. Does this make us any better than the rapist? The unborn child is an innocent bystander in the matter. The child didn't do anything wrong! Do you really want to kill the child? Do you really think it will make you feel better or make anyone feel any better? Will it change anything? Instead, how about I raise this child up to be a fine Christian and maybe even a doctor who saves lives or something like that. You know, make something really good happen from a very terrible situation. I wonder what Jesus would do ..... You know, he's the guy, who just loves little children .....

You know it is real easy to be a Christian when everything is going right, but it can be real hard when it's not. I have found, when in doubt, it is always good to go back to the basics. I believe, in the Roman Catholic religion, the only **"true"** religion, the basics would be referring to the ten commandments. The Lord does not say to choose one, two or more of the above to obey. He says you must obey "all" of them, "always", in "any" situation or all the time. You don't even get a medal or anything if you do, because he also says it's your "duty" and you don't get any medals for doing your duty. In other words it is expected of you to, at least, at the very least, to do your duty. When you are going to work, you don't get any medals for doing your job, it's your job you have to do it to get paid. Now if you do your job and go beyond the call of duty you may have something, other than that you are just doing your job. The commandments are the work you are entrusted with, your duty, period!

In the end you must "always" think of the unborn baby. God's miracle and gift to you. This child is no different than any other child with the exception it's tinier and hasn't had the privilege of being born as of yet. Would you kill a baby that was two months old? Of course not! What is the difference between a baby that will be born in two months and one already two months old? Age, size and the younger baby is not as fully developed yet. That is it! Let's take it a step farther. What is the difference between a baby who is two months old and one of four months? Age, size and the younger baby is not as fully developed as the older baby. Which, of the three babies, is it okay to kill? If you think it is okay to kill one, why not the other? If I have to answer that question for you, you have some real problems to deal with.

Think about the last analogy I gave you. It reeks of the truth! We, right now, are killing the youngest of those three babies and the only differences are age, size and the stage of development in their lives. Am I wrong? I will let "you" answer that question, all I ask is that you are honest and truthful. If I'm guessing right, we should all be thinking on the same level now. These are the things, which need to be said.

Legalized Murder (Oops ..... I Mean Pro-Choice)!

Man's law doesn't help, except for those who are, for a good percentage of the time, looking for an excuse to reverse their own promiscuity, yet another sin. Also, a way of ridding themselves of their responsibilities. No, no, no, our society is not the type of society that expects us to take responsibility for our own actions. It's legal, so I can have that abortion. These are the things you see and hear. Tell me I'm wrong. It's sick and it's nasty and it needs to end. Oh, that's right, we are not to speak of these things. We may "embarrass" someone. We should whisper. Man's law makes everything easier. WRONG! Man's law just helps to confuse the issue and gives us a "false" excuse to violate God's law.

There is one problem with that line of thinking. There are no excuses for violating God's law! NONE! Not to say you should violate man's law, but to say, when man's law is in conflict with God's law, you must follow that of the highest authority. God's law supercedes all laws! Man's law doesn't make everything okay and it should never be in conflict with God's law. They should always work in unison of each other.

I know you understand what I'm saying, but as I said in the beginning I'm going to say the things, which need to be said, but never seem to get said. All these things, which have been said, are things we already know. We are fooling ourselves and rationalizing ourselves right on the path to hell, when we spout out these foolish statements and we had better stop! It's getting ridiculous, it's been ridiculous! Are we waiting for the wrath of God to stop us from killing innocent babies?

I think it would be a very good idea not to wait that

long. I know we don't want to unleash the wrath of God, because by then it would be way too late. We should be very thankful the Lord is slow to anger. I believe we would all agree something must be done, but what? This will be the subject of the following section. Tune in and I will give you some of my ideas on the subject. We have to come together and defend our beliefs and be strong. At a bare minimum preserve our basic beliefs in faith and keeping man's law in check with those beliefs before they are taken away forever with no hope of ever getting them back.

Chapter 1A

Crusade #1,
Abolition of Abortion!

W e need to pull the lever, flip the switch or push the button. Whatever is necessary on the voting machines in your area to eliminate any elected official who supports pro-choice. Regardless of their platform otherwise! We have to do this as a group. We all have to be on the same page. There are approximately seventy million Roman Catholics and even more if you count Christians in general, who could, if we act as one, which by the way, is how the Lord expects us to act, eliminate this miscarriage of justice from the face of the earth forever!

Yes, it says Crusade #1. This would be a totally "non-violent" crusade with only one weapon, the voting booth. The number one indicates there are more to come. The abolition of abortion, murder, which I have deemed should be the first of our priorities, because lives are at stake

- - - - - - - - - - - - - -

Crusade #1, Abolition of Abortion!

every moment of each and every day, but there are more, which could and should be on the list and addressed. To give you an idea, the institution or sacrament of marriage, the family institution, stem cell research, euthanasia, homosexuality, freedom of speech to express our religion openly in this country, the land of the "free" and there could and should be more.

I see assaults in all these areas of our religion every day. Surely you must see it too. The moral decaying of our society even in the most basic areas, where us, older more seasoned citizens wouldn't have ever believed could have ensued as little as say twenty years ago. I think most everyone reading this book right now would agree with me. It has gotten completely out of hand. I have the strong feeling if no one stops it, it will end up being our demise.

First and utmost has to be the abolition of abortion! Our first crusade. This must be stopped as soon as possible. Every minute of every day the lives of our unborn babies is being taken. I give a lot of credit to the people out there you see picketing from time to time in front of the abortion clinics. I give them all the praise in the world. They are on the front lines of the battlefield! I feel they should continue in their efforts. They help to give the mothers of these unborn children a last chance, more or less, and any aid they will accept in making the morally correct decision before it's too late.

I must emphasize the fact that we need to act together to accomplish this feat. We have to be on the same page, all of us. If we do that, we can move mountains! The problem occurs when we are divided.

We need to have a plan. We need to be bold and let our

convictions be known. No more whispering! To do this right and to be really effective we need to hit them where it hurts at the voting booth. Let our elected officials know, through our churches, in every area of the country. We won't stand for it anymore! Republican, Democrat, Independent, it doesn't matter. If you support abortion, your not getting our vote, any of our votes! Your support for abortion "automatically" nullifies you! You better listen, because this is your warning.

We also need to organize ourselves. The perfect place being our churches. Yes, I know the Church can't endorse a candidate for public office and I will not suggest they do. We can discuss what issues are important to us as Roman Catholics and ask our members to look for those traits in the candidates they do choose. Then, get the word out to each and every member. The word being, vote as you will Democrat, Republican, Independent and so on, but "first" find out if your choice supports abortion. If they do, you adjust your vote accordingly and if necessary abstain from voting at all!

I will tell you this, you will never find me pulling the lever, flipping the switch, or pushing the button for any elected official supporting abortion. I will not have this on my record, on my conscience, a black spot on my soul to explain and justify to the Lord on judgement day! It will never happen! I'm a sinner just like the rest of us, but I guarantee "this sin" will not be on my soul!

If these elected officials know how devoted all of us are to the elimination of pro-choice, they will change. If they know they better change or be eliminated their platforms will start changing real fast. Oh yes, if they know their

Crusade #1, Abolition of Abortion!

jobs are on the line, they will redefine their positions quickly or be replaced. We have a lot of power to do good if we use it, but it has to be a joint effort. Now the question is, "How can we accomplish this?"

We need to start a "non-violent" crusade. A crusade for the abolition of abortion. Right now! We can do that with the power of our vote, this is our "secret" weapon. We have to do it before even that freedom and power is stripped away from us.

We need to speak loudly, no more "whisperings". We need to tell everyone around us and all our elected officials we won't stand for it any longer. We have had enough! We need to get out and draw the line. It is for our precious unborn babies people, please.

We need to let our elected officials know it doesn't matter what their platform is if it includes abortion, because abortion negates everything. Let them know, if you want our vote you had better toe the line and you better forget you even know the word abortion.

Whom has the power to change our laws? Our elected officials, so we have to concentrate our efforts on them. You have to go to the center of the problem. You can have all the good intentions in the world, but if you don't go where the problem is you don't get results.

To be really be effective you not only have to go to the elected officials, but to everyone. Don't be silenced! I do believe we still have freedom of speech in our country. There is no law, yet, saying you can't speak about your religion. No, you can't force anyone to listen, but you can bring what you have to say into the conversation. Let people know how you feel and why you feel the way you

Crusade #1, Abolition of Abortion!

do. If you explain "why", you just might convert them to our beliefs. Like I said before, there are a lot of things that should be said, but aren't. Maybe the person you speak to has never given enough thought about abortion. Maybe it is time he or she has. It can't hurt to try and it could be one more vote for our side, our crusade.

I try to always find a way of bringing our religion into my conversations with people. I do seem to be getting this bad taste in my mouth about freedom of speech. It appears everyone is gung ho about freedom of speech until the word God or Jesus comes into the conversation. This is all the reason I think we should speak more freely about our religion. Let people know it is okay. It also tells me we are doing too much whispering, when we should be shouting and praising with joy, all the wonderful things in our religion.

I fear religion is seldom talked about these days with our family, friends and even acquaintances. Religion shouldn't begin and end with Sunday mass. We need to wake people up and let them know what they are missing. I believe there are way too many people in our country, which are totally devoid of any religion whatsoever. I feel sorry for them and I do try to open their minds, so they may hear and see what they are missing. It could be no one ever took the time to explain to them the great mysteries of the world. How lonesome it must be to have no religion in your life. This just could be a reason for the next crusade after our crusade on the abolition of abortion.

If we get on track and come together as one we can get the job done and maybe educate and make aware to many people the importance of abolishing abortion. Maybe at

— — — — — — — — — — —

the same time expose people to our religion who maybe haven't had the privilege and create an interest in them to seek out more information or at least to ask questions.

Sometimes I think we don't realize how lucky we are to be so informed about our religion for our lives and our souls. Let us not keep our religion secretive. I think many people, especially these days, never have anyone sit down and just discuss religion. It could be all they need to help them to get started on the path of light, of truthfulness and righteousness. If you know someone like this, take the time and get them started. It is our duty not only to get ourselves to heaven, but everyone's.

I want to make it clear politics is not involved with this crusade. Your political affiliation or your elected official's party is irrelevant. What is relevant is your elected official's platform or stand on abortion. Democrat, Republican, Independent or any other party means nothing, its how they are going to represent our interests when it comes to the question of abortion. If they should decide that abortion is okay, then you know what you must do. I hope! Your vote, all our votes are important and if you let your elected officials know they won't be getting our votes if they are pro-abortion they will think twice before they vote against the people who put them in office in the first place. I'm not telling you to vote Democratic or Republican, but "against" abortion. If it means voting against a Republican, then so be it. If it means voting against an Independent, then so be it. If you are a Republican and you want my vote, at the very least, you better be pro-life and the same would apply to any other party. It's that important to me, to us, is what you would

- - - - - - - - - - - - - -

be telling your candidate, so you had better listen!

It doesn't take violence, it just takes a vote, your vote, everyone's vote to make this crusade happen. What better thing could you do, than become a part of a crusade to save the lives of the youngest, tiniest, most defenseless, soon to be citizens of our great nation. What a warrior you could be. A warrior without a sword or a gun fighting the good fight, saving the lives of millions of our babies.

We have a job to do. We need to rescue these babies in the name of common decency, in the name of the Lord! We can't allow this to continue. How can you explain this to your children? Do you tell them you don't care? What are they to think of us parents if we do nothing? What are they to think of our beliefs, our religion? Are you going to let your children think this is okay, this is normal, you need not worry about it? You should be thinking about these things. You are the parents, you need to have the answers for your children. They expect it of you.

There are many times I think we don't realize all the consequences of our actions. How do we explain these things, not only to our children, but our friends or anyone else? What do you say if someone asks you if your religion permits this, especially when you may have voted for an elected official who condones abortion? Can these things be ignored? Should they be ignored? We need to do some serious soul searching. We are the examples of society. We have responsibilities to our fellow man. We are disciples of our Lord Jesus Christ! Have we forgotten that? Do we even know or realize this? Is this just the job of our priests? Of our nuns?

We need to be asking ourselves a lot of questions like

this. I think it helps to wake us up and take notice. We need to show others what the right path is and explain the reasons we take the path we take. Help people to discern between right and wrong, good and evil. This is our duty as Christians and Roman Catholics.

In this particular battle time is of the essence. Time becomes one of the most precious things we have. We must make very good use of it. Literally every moment that goes by another child is murdered! Every moment counts! I know that sounds harsh and it should. It should be embarrassing! It should make us all hang our heads in shame and ask for forgiveness for allowing this to ever happen in this nation or anywhere. We are not doing our duty. What is worse is it is happening right in front of our eyes every day and no one seems to care, we just keep going on. We ignore it as if it is nothing to be concerned about. How can we be that way? How can we not care? It disgusts me to no end! We should be appalled!

Please consider what I have said. Take it to heart. There are little ones, babies who are counting on you and all of your friends. Please, don't let them down. Give them a chance to live their lives to the fullest like you and me. Give them your support, pray for our babies, do something really worthwhile in your life and help save theirs for the glory of our Lord Jesus Christ. Have a heart. This is from my heart to your heart and my heart is bleeding for desire to save these beautiful babies, our blood lines. Let not another drop of blood be spilled ..... Amen .....

Luke 6:31
Do to others as you would have them do to you.

- - - - - - - - - - - - - -

Chapter 1B

No, I Don't Hate You!

No, I don't hate you! I know there are some of you who have already had an abortion. I "do" hate your sin, but I "don't" hate you. Unfortunately, once done it can't be undone obviously. I have prayed for your unborn child as I have prayed for all of the unborn children. You should do the same. I don't hate you, but I'm deeply disappointed in you as I would be for anyone perpetrating such an act!

I sincerely hope and pray, because of the fact your reading this book right now, you are remorseful of the sin you have committed. You must realize, the gravity, the horrific nature, the eternal significance of your actions and certainly and above all be repentant!

I can't tell you the hurt I feel inside for your baby and everyone's baby who meets such a fate. They will always be in my daily prayers. I also have great sorrow for you. You will have to live with this in your heart and on your soul for the rest of your life. I can't even imagine how that

- - - - - - - - - - - - - - -

could possibly feel.

One of the side effects almost no one talks about is the pain, the hurt, the great sorrow many of the mothers feel after they have had an abortion. The results of their actions many times manifest themselves in their minds and drives many to a state of great depression knowing their acts are irreversible and could have been prevented. This is just one of the reasons I'm so adamant at stopping abortion before it is too late. Only they can truly describe the sorrow they feel. I can only imagine it must be almost as horrible as the act itself. I don't envy anyone going through such an ordeal.

I'm not forgetting the unborn baby! It goes without saying, their plight can be matched by no one. Abortion doesn't only affect the unborn, but "all" involved. Especially the mother, who is most intimately involved! Remember, as Roman Catholics we must forgive and show mercy to those who have fallen to sin. We are all sinners and not one mortal sin is any better than the other. I suggest we have all had mortal sins on our souls at one time or the other, so we should not cast any stones!

When there is an abortion there are victims'. Not one victim, but many. Many times we assume the baby is the only victim and with good reason. However, there are more. The parents of the mother should now be grandparents, but they are not. They have been cheated of their granddaughter or grandson. The aborted baby could have been your cousin, brother or sister. In which case, you have been cheated too. I haven't even mentioned the blood line of the aborted baby. The baby could have grown up and had children and those children could have had their children, but no more.

You see just one abortion has very far-reaching consequences and "everyone" suffers a loss in the families involved. This is another reason why abortion burns in my heart with such an appalling and nauseating fire. You probably can't even imagine all the possibilities of what could have been and should have been, but aren't, because of this abrupt and unnatural loss, which didn't even have to be! I believe any sane person, who really thought out all of the dire consequences of abortion, before the act was actually consummated, would never end up having the abortion in the first place. This is why these things need to be said. We all need to say these things to help those wrestling with the decision of abortion. We need to sit down and talk to them and explain to them the consequences of their actions.

Luke 23:34

"Father, forgive them, they know not what they do."

My suggestion to those who have had an abortion is to find a priest or nun as quick as humanly possible! Abortion is a "grave" sin and calls for excommunication from the Church. However, a priest will be able to tell you what must be done to have that action reversed. It can be reversed, but I suspect it will take great effort on your part. Not to mention a very contrite, remorseful and penitent state or posture of the mind and soul to say the least and most probably the use of a confessional with the willingness to do whatever penance deemed necessary. Clearly the Church does not take the act of abortion lightly and either should be anyone!

I have another suggestion. You will never be able to bring back your baby, but there may be something good, which can come from this great loss of yours. I'm sure you wouldn't want anyone to experience the feelings you have now. Feelings only you could possibly describe, because only someone who has gone through an experience such as this could imagine the sorrow, guilt and emptiness you must be feeling. Tell other expectant mothers, who may be considering abortion as an alternative and warn them of the consequences. Maybe, just maybe you could save an unborn baby yourself. Join the crusade, Crusade #1!

The closest thing I could think of to right a wrong as this, would be to help prevent the next abortion from happening. Prevent ten abortions from happening, save ten unborn children! The math is simple. It still won't bring back your child, but could you think of anything better to right this wrong? Show the love you really have for your child by never allowing this to happen again if at all possible.

We could use people who have experienced the worst of the worst. Who better to explain why abortion should never happen again, should never even be a choice! What is done is done. What we have to do is to look to the future and to prevent this from ever happening again. It wouldn't be easy. You would have to give all the lurid details and ensure they "really" know what they are getting themselves into, but it would be well worth the effort! To truly be effective you would have to bare your soul.

No, I Don't Hate You!

No one is perfect. Everyone makes mistakes. What I'm trying to do is to help you cope with the loss you are now feeling. I know it must be the most horrible thing you could imagine. Sometimes we don't realize the grave mistake we have made until it is too late.

Wouldn't it have been nice if someone would have come and explained all the significant, vast and egregious effects, which a decision to abort your baby entails? My guess is that never happened. They didn't want to embarrass you or your family. They were too busy whispering! In the mean time the deplorable procedure is accomplished and it is now too late.

Can you see how someone who has been through this may be able to say a few words, direct from their heart, that just may prevent this all from happening? Having experienced this yourself you would be able, like no one else, to explain the loss you are now feeling. A few words could be all it takes to save the life of an innocent unborn child and the grief, the sorrow, the mother will have to live with forever.

Our God is a forgiving God who is infinite in his mercy. Thank the Lord for that or we all would be in a lot of trouble! As a person who has already had an abortion you need to remember this and maybe even get some form of counseling.

Still yet another suggestion I have is the possibility of starting and setting aside a day of the year in memoriam for all the children whose lives have already been lost to abortion. What day would this be? A "smoke-free" day, a "green-day", an "earth-day or how about an "ABORTION-FREE" day! I don't know, but I have

- - - - - - - - - - - - - -

wrestled with the idea and a good date out of the year, not to interfere with other important dates and to stand alone and be revered on its own merits and importance is not easy to come up with. It would be a day of remembrance and prayer they most certainly deserve much like we remember the fallen soldiers of a war or the like. A holiday, to remember the lost lives of the unborn, who had "no-choice", who gave their lives, because of "our" trespasses.

This is a war! Right now we are losing the battle. The battle is claiming millions of lives of the innocent. This must change in the name of the Lord. The sooner we realize this and do something about it the better and we could move onto our next crusade. Oh, there are more things we need to get done, but this crusade, Crusade #1, has priority over everything else, because of the great loss of so many lives.

Maybe you could be the one who can come up with that perfect date, that perfect name and get the ball rolling and start organizing. Get everyone at your church and everyone you know to participate and set time aside for remembrance. Hopefully it would take off and everyone could get involved. Our fallen children deserve, at least as much. Wouldn't it be better than sitting in your Church and doing nothing?

Yes, there are things we can do. Things we should do. Things we should be doing already. We only need some people of conviction, desire and the initiative to leave that Church and set the example and let people know we will not stand for this anymore!

You, who have already felt the loss could be the first to

start this crusade and help save the lives of our future unborn children. If you and I don't do it, who will? The heart of this book is simply to wake people up and to take notice of what is going on right in front of their noses! This book is not for my sake or for the sake of money, but the sake of the children losing their lives every minute of every day!

We can all play a part in this war, but we need to do it as one. We can't stand on the sidelines any longer. There are babies depending on us. They are helpless! Whispering won't help. Sitting in Church and doing nothing, is not going to solve the problem. We actually have to get off our duffs and do something. The problem will not fix itself.

If I have to beg, than so be it. I'm begging you! Please! All of you please help. Now is the time! You say you would give your lives for your children. Prove it! We are all brothers and sisters here. The children lost are ours to save. The more who become involved and help, the quicker the war can be won and the fewer lives will be lost.

It will be easy to tell when we have done enough to save the unborn. It will be when no other baby dies by the knife in this country or anywhere else, before his or her full life is complete as determined by the will of our Lord. Let the Lord decide when our novels are complete. Don't play God yourself!

Let us do our duty to the Lord. Let us act like civilized human beings. Respect the sanctity of all our lives. It is written in our hearts and souls by our Lord.

We could just sit in our seats at Church and do nothing.

No, I Don't Hate You!
— — — — — — — — — — —

We could ignore abortion and hope it goes away by itself. We could be silent, so as not to stir up any trouble. We could make up all kinds of excuses for doing nothing at all. I sincerely hope we don't just sit there and do nothing and let our future generations be annihilated without lifting a finger. I hope we are better than that. I hope there is someone besides me who cares.

It would really disappoint me if we all just continue as before. I have faith in our wonderful religion and these great United States of America, "One Nation, under God", that we can and will do what it takes to save our babies. I don't know what I will do next if nothing happens. I will say this, I personally will not just sit in that pew in Church and do nothing again. I wouldn't be able to stand myself if I did. If this doesn't work, I will try something else, I'm not sure what I will do, but I will not be happy until we save our future brothers and sisters from this travesty of man's law.

Have you ever imagined what our earth would be like if all we did was to follow the ten commandments the Lord gave us without fail? We wouldn't have to lock the doors of our houses. We wouldn't have to lock up our cars. We wouldn't have to ask for help. Everyone would be our friend, our brother or sister to come to our aid in time of need. We wouldn't need prisons, Everyone would be speaking the truth. Families would be living in harmony. There would be no divorce, no cursing. Maybe, just maybe this is why our Lord gave us these commandments. Maybe, so he would have a civilized world of decent people to bring into heaven with him. Last, but not least and above all, there would be no murder, even of the unborn ..... Amen.

Chapter 2

Red Flag - National Healthcare Plan!

How in the world can you expect anyone who has no respect for the sanctity of life to develop a healthcare plan that does? What do you expect? Unbelievable! I will tell you on paper it sounds really good. Healthcare for everyone! I don't really think anyone with any kind of compassion whatsoever could have any problem with everyone in our country having healthcare. The problem herein lies with whom you are going to put in charge of instituting such a plan and finding the resources necessary to pay for the plan.

You don't put a convicted burglar in charge of running a bank. You don't put a convicted drug trafficker in charge of operating a pharmacy. If you expect this healthcare plan to respect the lives of all its patrons, you don't put anyone, but anyone in charge who openly has no regard for life and its sacredness. Do you? I know I wouldn't want anyone in

- - - - - - - - - - - - - - -

charge of my healthcare plan unless he has nothing but the utmost regard for the lives of its members at the minimum! Is this person a politician? I think not!

Have you been watching the politicians lately in this country? I don't know about you, but Capital Hill seems nothing more than an abyss of corruption to me. I'm not saying there are only bad politicians out there, but the good ones seem to be getting real hard to find. You want to put the government in charge of a national healthcare plan? Have you seen how they have ran the post office, the social security office, veteran's hospitals, Fannie Mae, Freddy Mac and medicare? Give me a break! I'm no genius, but it appears the governments' track record for running any kind of institution leaves a little bit to be desired.

This is where the first "red flag" should come up. Notice I said the "first". I'm seeing plenty of red with this plan. The persons put in charge is just the tip of the iceberg. The two-thousand page bill is next on the list!

Lately the congressmen we have, have been giving me some nightmares. They are passing bills through without even reading what is in them! Need I say anything more? I hate to say this, but any congressman who signs a bill without reading it loses all my respect! A congressman who pushes a bill through at 2:00 a.m. on Christmas Eve doesn't thrill me either. I hear one congressman say this provision is in the bill and another one saying it isn't. How can they possibly know? They haven't read the bill! No one had the time to read the two thousand pages in the bill, because they are pushing it through like a locomotive on steroids! Why does this have to happen in the wee hours

- - - - - - - - - - - - -

Red Flag - National Healthcare Plan!

— — — — — — — — — — —

of the morning while everyone is sleeping? Red flags, red flags, red flags, red flags and more red flags! What is going on here? Is there nothing here, which seems to be a bit shady in its operation? Is anyone paying attention to these congressman? You are going to let them in charge of everyone's healthcare plan?

These congressmen are getting away with murder here, in more ways than one! Does the healthcare bill include a provision to have taxpayers payed abortions for women? How can anyone possibly know? Some more red flags. Actually, I think some people do know, but we are not one of them! In other words, I believe we are being hoodwinked. My head is just about ready to explode! If you have read this book from the beginning you know my main concern is with abortion, but it isn't my only concern. This particular bill brings to light many more concerns of mine. I'm afraid our unborn babies are really in trouble with this bill and there is a good chance many more besides them.

I have been hearing a lot of rumors going around and I will tell you the truth I'm really getting scared. Not so much for me, but for my fellow man. It just may be, many of these so-called rumors, may not really be rumors at all.

Unfortunately, I believe by the time this book comes out this healthcare bill will have already been through the wringer and either been passed through or not, hopefully not! I say this only, because there is a lot more we need to know about the contents of its two thousand pages first. I really can't comprehend how anyone, especially our congressman, could even dream of passing a bill such as this without, at the very minimum, of going through it

- - - - - - - - - - - - - -

with a fine-toothed comb. What more important things do they have to do? We are talking about a bill which encompasses approximately one sixth of the nation's economy! If that isn't enough, you start paying for it four years before you receive any benefits from it. Who is paying for it? You are! Why the rush! If it doesn't take effect for another four years, how about we take our time and try to do it right.

Something smells fishy in Denmark here. Maybe, just maybe they are trying to slide some very questionable things right under our noses they know we won't appreciate. I'm getting a very bad taste in my mouth again. I believe prudence should tell us we need to examine every line of this bill or we are going to be sorry. Once it has passed, it will probably take an act of God too undue what is already done if need be.

I would like to discuss some of the possible issues here with you now, hopefully before it is too late. It won't be easy to do, because we are only getting bits and pieces of what we think is or isn't in the bill. I mean to say, if congress isn't going to read the bill, maybe we can! There are some really big issues to deal with here. Too big to just sign off on. I don't know about you, but I don't appreciate this sleight-of-hand congress is trying to pass off on us, it just seems too sneaky to me.

Now I know a lot of you have your hands full just trying to make ends meet with our economy the way it is. It isn't easy in today's world to keep a household going for many. However, we can't let these congressmen snooker us and catch us with our pants down or who knows what we will have to deal with for the near future and even beyond.

We have to be very vigilant and cautious or the United States will no longer be what it was, or what we hoped it would be. I speak mainly in regards to our faith and what we believe. You don't want to wake up tomorrow morning living in a whole new country with the same name disrespecting the laws of God. I hope not anyway! I get the feeling the rug is being pulled right out from under us and if we do nothing we will be very sorry.

Now, to start with, lets talk about the abortion issue in this new healthcare plan. You know this is my pet issue. As of now it is quite unclear what to believe. I hear from one side there will be no funding of abortion and from the other side it is said funding for abortion is in the bill, but we just won't call it that. You know, we wouldn't want to get anyone upset or even embarrass anyone.

I have the gut feeling inside federal abortion funding could very well be included. You might ask, "Why would you ever think that?" First of all my guesses is this kind of legislation would not be very popular with the population as a whole, so if we are going to try to pass this type of bill we could make it very confusing and get it lost in a mass of two thousand pages. By the way, most bills take much less than two thousand pages to be presented to congress, much less, say like fifteen, sixteen or seventeen hundred less! Next, I wouldn't call it abortion funding, I would give it a different name and then we will send it through so fast no one will have time to read the bill before they sign it. Finally, I would see it is passed at one or two in the morning on Christmas Eve, when no one is paying any attention to it. Do you see where I'm coming from here?

Could it be any more obvious? It is possible I'm totally wrong, but then who knows, after all no one has had the time to read the bill!

If you had a lawyer and you told him you signed a contract without reading it, what do you think he would say? Do you think he would say, "Don't worry about it everything will come out all right?" No, he wouldn't say that at all, he would say you must be some kind of fool or something! This is why I'm losing respect for these congressmen. Most of them are lawyers themselves and I know they know better. Maybe they just don't care?

I will be fraught with extreme grief if indeed abortion funding is included in this bill. I can't stand, even the thought, that my hard earned tax dollars could be going for abortion of which I detest so much. This would include you too! Does this meet with your approval? I certainly hope not, but keep sitting in your chair and sipping your coffee and that just may be what happens like it or not. I know it wouldn't be easy. I'm sure, like everyone else, your schedules are full, but you need to take the time and make the time or they could destroy the United States you know and love.

Everyone needs to get actively involved or nothing will happen. You need to be aware of what is going on around you. You can't keep walking with blinders on. If you do, I can almost guarantee you will be sorry. There is a lot of evil out there and you need to get up and do something about it or not only will it live on, but it will get worse.

Oh, I'm not done, there is more in this bill you should be aware of. We are just breaking the ice here. If abortion wouldn't be enough to worry about, there are other things we need to be concerned with.

Next comes the death panel, oh, I'm sorry, the "advisory" panel. We don't want to get anyone upset. These are the people who will decide if you are "worthy" of healthcare. You see when you get older is it really advantageous to society that they should spend thousands, maybe tens of thousands, of dollars to keep you alive, when you probably only have a few good years left anyway? Do you really want to take advantage of our society this way? Well, worry not, the advisory panel will decide for you. They will make the determination if the money spent is worth the effort. You know, why spend thousands of dollars just to give you maybe only six months or even a year or two longer life. How can you think to put such a burden on society?

Is this what you want? Did you read the last paragraph real carefully? I hope you're not very old, because this could be the new up and coming events to your block in the near future. It could be, but we just don't know for sure, because you see no one has really read the bill in its entirety yet, so relax. This is just a suggestion of mine, but maybe we should take the time to read the bill, you know, just as kind of a precaution.

I hope you realize I'm making light of the possibilities here. There are rumors, however. Why rumors? Rumors, because we don't read bills anymore, we just sign them! Are you prepared for the possibilities? Can you see what could be happening here, could be, because we are just signing this bill, not actually reading it or anything like that. You can get all this without really trying. All you have to do is sit in your easy chair and sip your coffee.

- - - - - - - - - - - - - -

That's it, nothing else! What's the worst that could happen
.....

Let's talk a little about this advisory panel. Who are these people? Well, we don't know that either. Since this would be a government operation, it wouldn't surprise me if they are appointed by someone up the chain of command. They could be anyone I would suppose. Let's see if we could figure on how this might work.

This panel could be very interesting, because we won't have any idea what rules they are going by or who is making the rules. We are going to have to use a couple of "what ifs" to see if we can figure this operation out. "What ifs", can be a good thing used to kind of give a feel of what could happen or what might happen.

Let's start with, what if your grandfather is seventy nine years old and needs an operation on his heart? Well, the operation is going to be expensive, probably about thirty or thirty-five thousand dollars to perform. This is going to mean a visit to the panel to see if and when you can be treated. So, you go before the panel and make your case and then they convene to make their decision. Oh, you go there with your family for, lets say, some moral support, as you all await the panel's decision. After some time has past, they come back and say, "We have looked over the case and we are sorry to say we have determined the cost of the operation far exceeds the benefits received, so we are going to have to decline your request." Next!

Now what? Remember this is "your" grandfather! What do you say to him? Sorry you are going to cost society too much to keep alive, so we will just make things real cozy for you at home. Have a seat in your favorite chair and we will get you your slippers and something to drink. We did all that we could do. Too bad, you just missed the cut-off point.

What if you went somewhere else with your grandfather? Oh, that's right, there is no where else to go. It's like the social security office. If you had some trouble in receiving your benefits at the social security office, can you go to some other office to get a little satisfaction? I don't think so.

Can you appeal the panel's decision? After all this is your grandfather! What if you are stuck with their decision no matter what? Are you going to have to go to another country and see what happens there? If your grandfather gets his heart operation, everything will be fine. There must be something we can do. Is this panel's decision final?

What if the panel says the operation is okay, but he has to get on a waiting list and it will be about a year and a half before the operation can be scheduled? However, your grandfather is in really bad shape and there is no way he could possibly wait that long. Maybe we could get him bumped up on the list and get the operation sooner? What if the rules say once a determination is made its final? Remember, we are now dealing with a government agency, not a private doctor anymore.

What if we get another opinion? They always say when you go to a doctor and get a diagnosis, you should always go to another for a second opinion. I don't know, somehow I think a government run advisory board or panel isn't going to have time to deal with these kinds of things. Of course, no one has really read the bill, so who knows? I guess we will find out once the bill is passed.

What if a guy on the board or panel simply just doesn't like your grandfather's looks and he votes no to the operation and he is the deciding vote? Does the panel have to give you a reason for their decision? What goes into the process of making the decision anyway? Is money the only factor? Is it the expected prognosis of the patient after an operation of this type is performed? Is it the availability of the necessary staff to perform the operation?

Who gets on these panels anyway? Is it anyone off the street? Must they be doctors? What rules do they go by? Are there any rules? If there are rules, who is in charge of making them? If there are rules, can they be changed? Who is in charge of picking the members of these panels? What credentials does he or she have?

You know, your grandfather still hasn't had his operation. Is this how it all ends? Some board decides when it is all over for your grandfather. What if it wasn't your grandfather? What if it was you? What if "you" are the grandfather or maybe the grandmother?

Shouldn't we be discussing these things? Like right now! Maybe before this kind of government bureaucracy goes into effect. Maybe the politician's know what's best for all of us. We could just leave it in their hands to decide. They only wish the finest for us right? I'm getting that bad taste in my mouth again.

This is where we are heading people. Is this what you really want? It is one thing to want healthcare for everyone, but do we want it at any cost? Do we want boards to decide our fate? Is this the healthcare reform we have all been waiting for? You may have noticed I have

— — — — — — — — — —

asked many questions in this example. I did that, because I suspect others might ask a lot of the same type questions. I think they all would be reasonable questions to ask considering the situation. There is one particular question I purposely left out. Do you have any idea what that might be?

You could ask all the questions I have asked here and probably plenty more. All would be reasonable when you are considering the lives of people. It would appear your life rests in their hands. A simple yea or nay could be the biggest thing you have ever faced in your life. It seems to me, that is a lot of power to give to a government bureaucracy. Yet, I have left one of the most important things out! Have you guessed it yet?

What if in this panel's decision the sanctity of life is "not" considered? Will it even be discussed? This is what frightens me the most. Are we so callous, are we people that don't even take the sanctity of life into consideration anymore? Is it just the money that matters? Is it just the burden your putting on society? Can you see where the term "death panel" might come from? I know it is a harsh thing to say and quite "embarrassing" even. I guess we could give it another name. How about advisory board? Yes, that sounds much better. With a name like that it can't be all bad, right?

Are we to accept healthcare for everyone at all costs? Do we throw everything we believe in away simply to say we have healthcare for any and everyone? Do we just disregard the sanctity of life? Like I said in the beginning, healthcare for everyone sounds real good on paper, but what really matters will be how it is achieved, at least in

- - - - - - - - - - - - - -

- - - - - - - - - - - -

my personal opinion. Keep in mind right now, as I speak, anyone in need of emergency healthcare can go to the emergency room of any hospital and by law must be treated. Anyone! Insured or not! It's the law!

Yes, I really think we ought to rush this bill through before it's too late. This way we could all rest easy knowing there is healthcare for everyone. It should cure all our healthcare problems from this point on. Yea right! Are we crazy? Topping everything off we aren't even going to read the fine print. We're simply going to let it in the hands of our esteemed politicians. Thank goodness they are trying to put this bill through before the state of the union speech comes out! It might even be used to credit someone's legacy. Whew. Talk about great timing! Free healthcare for everyone! Well, okay, maybe not exactly free. Hmmm ..... Maybe we should discuss how this may be paid for. Now I hope we all know any institutions from the government don't always come at a cheapest of prices. We do know where all the government's money comes from, right? That is correct. It comes from us, the taxpayers. We really should discuss this too, since it does involve one sixth or thereabouts of the entire economy. We will make this our next topic of discussion.

It is rumored we will start paying for this plan immediately even though we receive no benefits from it for about four years. It was also supposed to cover everyone, but it's rumored and seems to have left out about eighteen million people. Oops! Yes, all these rumors again, because we haven't read the bill yet. Oh boy, this bill is just going to be chalk full of surprises for us all! Who knows where all of this could lead us.

- - - - - - - - - - - - - -

Red Flag - National Healthcare Plan!

— — — — — — — — — — —

I hate to be the bearer of bad news, so I will tell you the scuttlebutt also declares once the healthcare plan is in full operation the costs will balance out and everyone will break-even money wise. If you believe that, I have some swamp land in Florida I would like to sell you.

I may have forgotten to mention everyone will have healthcare whether you want it or not. Meaning you will be required to purchase it and if not you will be fined and who knows maybe even be imprisoned. Believe it or not, some people don't care to have a healthcare plan. Most are young and feel it's unnecessary for them to have it presently, but maybe in the future as they get older they would change their minds. However, to institute this particular healthcare plan it seems it is necessary everyone is a participant in order for it to work properly. Henceforth, the requirement to purchase the plan is a necessity.

Some say you will not have to change to the government healthcare plan if you are happy with the plan you have now. Then, there are some, who say that isn't true, everyone will eventually have to be on the government healthcare plan. It seems only a select few are privy to what exactly is in this healthcare plan.

It's said the final negotiations on this plan will be seen on C-SPAN, so everyone will know what is really going on. Oops, I forgot, they changed their mind about that and the final negotiating on the terms of the plan will be behind closed doors. I wonder what happened there? They wouldn't be trying to hide anything would they?

Before I forget, there seems to be this thing on euthanasia in the plan. I haven't heard any real details on that. It must be of no real consequence I guess. Then again, maybe that is something someone should be looking into also. All of a sudden this whole plan is getting pretty complicated to sort out. Maybe we should slow things down a bit and look a little deeper into what this plan encompasses. We wouldn't want to make any hasty decisions when we are talking about the lives of our people, our brothers and sisters.

I have raced through this healthcare plan to give you an idea of some of the major points and considerations. The money aspect of the plan is important, but what concerns me the most are the issues on human life. Abortion tops my personal list, but there is much more as you can see. I truly respect the idea for healthcare for everyone, but not at any cost! We have to be extremely careful about what is ensuing. Violation of many of our beliefs and basic God given rights could be thrown right out the door. The politics of the matter means nothing if you give away your religious beliefs. I'm talking about the basics here, the ten commandments.

The biggest red flag you can find is as soon as you see where one of the commandments is going to be or even possibly be violated. This is our standard to go by, provided by our good Lord. If you use that as your standard it is really quite easy to make the right decisions in our life. If you let anyone take these away, you have lost the battle, in fact the war.

Every once in a while you have to sit back and look at the entire forest. We truly can't see the forest for the trees. We are becoming a society totally consumed and engrossed in our little worlds and our daily lives we never look up to see the entire picture. If we continue, we are going to follow that Pied Piper right into the drink and never realize what has happened until it is too late.

All this can be cured at the ballot box. We need to be aware of what is going on around us and take some initiative to do something about it. It's not party affiliation we are concerned with, it's the party platform. We need to elect those legislators who have respect for the sanctity of life and our God given commandments. Those legislators who are already in office need to be checked on their voting records. With the advent of the internet, that particular task becomes much easier.

We need to come together with this information and meet in our Church halls and meeting rooms. As I have said before we can do a lot together as a group. We need to eliminate those running for office from our choices when voting if their platforms will violate the Natural Law, the laws of God and our unalienable rights as citizens of these great United States as stated in "The Declaration of Independence." I know we must have all heard our rights to "life" (no abortion), liberty and the pursuit of happiness. They have already taken away the lives and rights of multitudes of our unborn babies through abortion! Do we let them take away the rest of our rights?

Do you want all the rights and freedoms our soldiers and sailors died for to be in vain? All it could take is one 2:00 a.m. session of congress to do it! Let us try to keep this as "One Nation, under God". Let us be the examples. Let us show our brothers and sisters the path of light and righteousness. Help to lead your congregation in this battle for the glory of God. It's our duty.

- - - - - - - - - - - - - - -

Red Flag - National Healthcare Plan!

Look at all the evil in our country. We are bombarded by it daily. We need to draw a line somewhere so our citizen's can lead normal and decent lives. I feel this is the greatest nation under the sun in spite of all the inequities and transgressions, because we are clinging onto our beliefs in God. However, I believe our grip on God is loosening up and we need to tighten it again. If we lose our grip on God, we have lost everything! We need to unite and see that we never lose sight of our Lord. Time is of the essence! It doesn't take long to lose everything. If you procrastinate, it will only make matters worse if not almost impossible to fix.

I see everything slipping away real fast, which is part of my inspiration in this writing. My concern is not with global warming or climate change nearly as much as it is with our souls. A clean planet and a dirty soul don't appeal to me. Our priorities need to be re-examined. In fact, our priorities could very well be the subject for another book. Many times I see things and wonder if anyone makes note of any priorities whatsoever. It almost seems as we are lost in a maze and are oblivious to anything of any real importance in our lives. To cite an example: I will see someone get in a car accident and the first thing he asks is if there is any damage? Not, is anyone hurt?

Priorities are exactly what we need here! As Roman Catholics our number one priority is the Lord and his will and then we go from there. I know as you read these things you must be saying everyone knows that. I would think so myself until I see how our own members vote and the people we elect or how our prestigious Roman Catholic universities give honorary degrees out to someone who clearly advocates abortion, even partial birth abortion! What do I think then? Maybe what I'm saying, as obvious as it is, needs to be said. Maybe we should be reminded of these things?

I hear a leader in congress, a "big" abortion enthusiast, claiming she is a Roman Catholic. Please do me a favor, if you are pro-abortion, please don't insult me by calling yourself a Roman Catholic! Personally, I don't want to be associated with you until you clean up your act. Things like this totally disgust me! All I hear is silence. The silence in the air deafening! No one says a thing! Yes, sometimes I'm embarrassed to be a Roman Catholic, not because of my beliefs, but because of the actions of my fellow Roman Catholics!

I happen to discuss our religion at work and with friends all the time and these associates of mine already know a lot of the beliefs of the Roman Catholic Church, because I have my ways of integrating it into the conversations. I think many of them know more now about the Roman Catholic faith than their own. Many times at work I will play some religious trivia and ask them questions like what is the fourth commandment or when is the next religious holiday or anything along those lines just to spark some interest. Now, when they hear some of the things I stated earlier, they ask me questions like: "I thought you said Roman Catholics didn't believe in abortion?" It's embarrassing! What am I supposed to say them? Do I tell them some don't and some do? I shouldn't even have to deal with this!

Actually, I have to deal with this often. I tell them, make no mistake, the Roman Catholic religion does not and never will support abortion in any way, shape or form. Should I even have to make this statement? No, I shouldn't, but I do to make sure the record is set straight. We need to get back on the ball. We are getting off track and we need to do something about it. No matter what, I'm going to try to keep saying the things that need to be said, but never get said, but should be. I will be the first to admit I'm scared and you should be too. Everyone needs to participate, to help, please .....

Chapter 3

Attacked From All Directions!

I would like to say the only problems we have to deal with would be the ones previously mentioned. What I would like to say and what I have to say are going to be two different things. We are getting assaulted from every direction. It would appear in our country it isn't very popular to be Christian anymore.

Everywhere there are signs of this attack on Christians taking place. I'm not talking physical attacks, but attacks on our beliefs, customs and traditions. There is evidence of it everywhere. I know, you know what I'm talking about. I will say it anyway, because I feel it's my duty to say the things that should be said, but never seem to get said.

Actually, I do hear them being said, but more in a whisper than anything else. I think we are so scared to offend anyone or to be politically incorrect we are letting anyone do whatever they want, even if it rips apart our customs, our beliefs and our coveted traditions. Part of the problem lies in the fact I believe it's our nature to be agreeable and to let people do as they will. I don't necessarily think this to be a bad thing generally. At the same time I feel we have rights like anyone else. I'm talking about our Christian beliefs, our customs and our wonderful traditions.

I hope this doesn't sound bad and I hope I don't offend anyone, but I believe in the old saying, "when in Rome, do as the Romans do". I think what I'm going to ask is very reasonable, I hope you feel the same.

First, may it be stated I totally enjoy the fact we have many people immigrating here, to the great United States of America. I can understand people wanting to come to our great nation. Personally I love asking new immigrants all kinds of questions about where they are from, their customs, about the different foods they eat and even try to understand a little of their languages. I have no problem with that whatsoever. In fact it makes for some very interesting conversations.

If you remember, I always like to put myself in the other person's shoes when I make decisions. I will try to do the same here and we will see what happens.

I have traveled to many countries in the past and I find them all to have very distinct characteristics, customs and laws. I love traveling to other countries, every place always seems to have some fascinating feature or features and very wonderful and friendly people. When I go to these countries I feel I'm their guest and should act appropriately.

Attacked From All Directions!

I feel I have to respect their way of doing things. I would never even dream of trying to change their ways. After all their customs, traditions and their general way of life are what makes them so interesting in my eyes. If every country I visited was the same as ours, what would be the point of going there? Just because they are different doesn't mean they are bad or wrong. Above all, I'm a visitor, a guest. I have no right to expect them to do anything differently simply because I showed up.

Taking it a step further, if I were to decide to move to one of these countries I would do so with the thought if I move there I will have to conform to their ways of doing things. Not the other way around! I wouldn't expect them to change anything to please me. They didn't come to me. I came to them. If your going to live here, you have to live our way. Not to say I couldn't do anything the way I use to as long as it doesn't interfere with their customs or laws.

Doesn't that way of thinking sound reasonable to you? I wouldn't want to force myself or my ways on anyone and I wouldn't want anyone to force themselves or their ways on me. It seems like a fair trade off to me.

I told you all that, just to tell you this. The Christians in this country have customs and beliefs they have observed, most from the very start of this nation and not just Christians, but all of us. I'm mainly concerned with our Christian customs, but you can take any of them. What I resent is when immigrants come in and make hay with our customs and traditions. I wouldn't expect to do that in their country and I don't think they should expect to do it in ours.

- - - - - - - - - - - - - - -

Attacked From All Directions!

- - - - - - - - - - - -

Should we be expected to change our beliefs, our customs and traditions for every new person who decides to visit or reside here? Some of these customs we have had for forty, fifty and even some for over a hundred years and more. I want to be very cordial to our new guests and residents. I don't have a problem with them observing their customs in our country as long as they don't violate any of our laws or infringe on our ways of doing things. As much as I want to respect their ways of doing things, I expect them to respect our ways of doing things.

This is all I'm asking. I suspect immigrants come to the United States because of the way we are, for freedom, for the opportunities and many other wonderful reasons. I believe if they come here they should expect to conform to our ways of doing things. Just the same, if we go to other countries to visit or live we should expect to conform to that country's ways of doing things.

Mutual respect for each others country is all I ask. I really don't want to say if you don't like our laws, rules and customs maybe you shouldn't be here, but maybe I have to. Looking from the other direction, if I don't like a particular country's laws and customs, I might visit there, but I definitely wouldn't try to live there. Above all, I wouldn't go there to live and expect them to change all their rules and customs to suit me. If I would go there to live, I would expect "I" would have to do the changing not them!

I really want the immigrants to this country to see us as a very friendly and loving nation. I want them to be glad they made the trip. I think if we have mutual respect for each other there is no reason for there to be any problems

- - - - - - - - - - - - - -

at all.

What I have explained to you is what comes from the heart. I always try to be fair and expect to be treated likewise. To my chagrin, I do not feel this is what is happening. Yes, I'm getting that bad taste in my mouth again. I feel our beautiful traditions, customs and beliefs are being stripped from us. There is silence, at least for the most part. We do nothing. I sincerely hope I'm not the only one who feels this way. I don't want to feel bad when I say God in public. I don't want to feel bad when I say the word Christmas, because it has the name Christ in it. I don't want to feel bad when I tell people I have to go to Church on Sunday. I don't want to feel bad when I tell people I pray regularly. All my life I have been doing these things, saying these things and now all of a sudden they are bad? There is still freedom of speech right? Does freedom of speech apply to everything, but religion?

What is wrong with this picture? What is happening to our country? Isn't anyone going to do anything? I can't believe I even have to talk about these things. These things should be a given. What is happening here? Hello! Laying back in our easy chair with our feet propped up on the ottoman isn't working anymore! Am I having another one of those nightmares? Are we going to let all our beliefs, customs, ceremonies, practices, heritage and traditions get striped from us one by one? There disappearing day after day, one after another and I wait and wait and no one does a thing. Yes, I'm guilty too! However, I'm getting sick of it! Shouldn't all of us be? Things are going way too far out of hand.

I think there is a point in time where we have to put a

stop to all this. I can't imagine what is going to happen if we let it go very much farther. It is already much farther than I would have ever believed it could be. It seems as though we have lost all sight of common decency and in particular our beliefs.

I don't see this ever stopping unless someone puts their foot down and says this is it, we have had enough! I can't live this way anymore. I don't want to live this way anymore. Am I speaking to the wall or is there anyone else who feels the same? I can only speak for the people directly around me, but I know they all feel the same, so I'm guessing there are others.

I thought it was so bad years ago, but it wasn't nothing like this. It definitely wasn't perfect back then, but I still feel it was nowhere near as bad as it is now. I have seen plenty of God-fearing people then, but now, not too much. Not only does it scare me, but it makes me sad. How lonely it must be not to know of God or not to believe. We need to try and fix that problem amongst many of our problems.

If we are going to live here, we need to do our best to make this the best country in the world. Let people see what "One Nation, under God" really means. We need to get them to understand it is a way of life, not just a slogan. I have no doubt we can do it, but we have to do it together and be smart about it. Roman Catholics, above all, should be leading the way. We are about twenty million strong in the United States and we can flex our muscles if we have a mind to. I have faith, I know we can!

In the next few sections I will better explain where we might be losing the battle and discussing what we might do to fix that problem. I know you have seen or heard what is coming. You would have to be living in a cave somewhere not to. The real question is what to do about it and I will offer up some suggestions to start with.

I hate to present problems without, at the very least, offering up some kind of solution to those problems. I think you will agree with me there are a lot of things that need fixing and sometimes it can feel hopeless trying to make any changes. I think if we take it a day at a time, a step at a time we can make some headway. There may be a few small steps at first, but I think once we really get the ball rolling we can do some cruising.

Stay tuned in for the following. We have to do this together and the sooner the better. The way it appears to me is there is a mold growing in our country supporting an unbearable stench and it is slowly, but deliberately consuming or encroaching on everything we hold dear to our hearts. Much like that mold you find at times in our basements and if you do nothing about it, it just gets worse and never goes away. This mold is meandering its way through our country little by little, through our heritage, traditions, beliefs, customs, schools, families and even churches. It is really beginning to affect almost every aspect of our lives and in my belief taking us farther and farther off the path of light and righteousness.

I believe it not only needs to be contained, but also eliminated. You wouldn't let a mold continue in your basement with the stench and destruction it causes. The same should be true with this mold filtering through our country. First we need to identify it and then halt it in its tracks or we will be consumed, as being afflicted with some disease, by it.

The issues I speak of can't be cured overnight. It will take some time to eradicate their effects. They didn't appear overnight and their fires won't be extinguished overnight, but you need to start somewhere and now is as good a time as any. The longer we wait, the tougher it will be to halt them in their tracks. We are being attacked from all directions, on every front! If we work together on this as in the abortion issue we can clean up the mess in this country and make it stronger and better than ever before.

Chapter 3A

Assault on the American Flag!

This mold, this disease begins with an assault on the American flag, our flag! Previously I told you a good way to discern between right and wrong would be to use the ten commandments as a standard to measure everything else by and I stand by that now. When in doubt the ten commandments are always something you can count on.

Next comes the Declaration of Independence, the Constitution and the Pledge of Allegiance, at least when we are referring to our country. I believe these three documents are the keys to our country's success and the standard we should use in defending and maintaining our beliefs, rights and laws.

One of my favorite lines or phrases is in the Pledge of Allegiance as you may have already figured out. "One Nation, under God", Is something I hold near and dear to my heart. I love that line! It tells me I'm living in the right place. What better country could you live in? A country which respects' God and all he stands for. I know of no other nation which makes that claim and it suits me fine.

In 1954 President Eisenhower in response to the communist threat of the time urged Congress to add the words "under God", which produced the thirty-one word pledge we use today. The year I was born, how fantastic is that!

Here is where the mold begins spreading its stench and disease! There are people who want to take this part of the Pledge of Allegiance away! It has been there now for fifty-five years! Are we to let this happen? Not if I can help it! This is where our country is going, this is the kind of thing I have been talking about. They want to take our God away! I say, "No Way!" What is the United States of America coming to, to allow something like this to happen? I know, it hasn't happened yet, but you better not give these people the chance or it will!

We have the Declaration of Independence and the line: "We hold these truths to be self-evident, that all men are created equal, that they are endowed by their Creator with certain unalienable Rights, that among these are Life, Liberty and the pursuit of Happiness." Do we also have to get rid of the word "Creator"? Give them a chance and that probably will be gone too, along with our unalienable rights! They have already gotten rid of the right of "Life", when it comes to our unborn babies. They have replaced it with "Choice"! Talk about an assault on the flag and what it stands for.

Finally, the Constitution, which I like to look at as the ten commandments of our government. If we follow the

Constitution to the letter, everything else seems to fall into place. Guess what? We don't! Our own government has been violating it for years, especially in these days! They want this new healthcare plan made so you must buy in or get fined. Constitutional? I think not! If the healthcare plan should go through, you can bet you will have to purchase it.

The mold grows and grows and grows. It continues through every aspect of our lives. We need to clean it up before it destroys everything this great country is built on, it's very foundation. Our Founding Fathers were a pretty smart bunch. Our soldiers and sailors have fought for the words in these documents, some even giving their lives. If we do nothing, we show a great disrespect for all they have achieved.

The words of these documents are one thing and I appreciate them dearly, but there is something more important than the words themselves. The most important thing is what the words stand for, what they represent. You take them away and you have nothing.

Like it or not, this great nation was founded on Christian beliefs. There can be no argument here. It is our history and it is a fact! You can argue with the facts, but you can't change the facts, facts are facts. Do you really want any and everyone who wants to, to upset the very foundation this country was built on?

Why do you suppose we have all the immigrants to this nation, both legal or illegal coming to this country? We have them coming in by the herds! Do you think they are coming here by the droves because we are a cruel, wicked and a barbaric nation?

Assault on the American Flag!

They come here because we are a land of opportunity for the pursuit of happiness and freedom, both of speech and religion. We respect the rights of individuals and provide justice for all. We have our military, the best in the world, to protect us from evil nations, terrorism and to protect our "God" given rights. This is why people come here in multitudes. Don't let anyone tell you differently.

I love being a part of a nation like this! No, it isn't perfect, but I have done a lot of traveling in my days and I haven't seen any other country that has come close, well, except for Vatican City (Holy See), the smallest "country" on earth.

Vatican City is a story in itself. It is a sovereign and independent country completely contained within the borders of Rome. It has a population of a little over eight hundred people and no highways, just city streets. The Pope is in charge of everything legal, executive and judicially. The only real problem I see is that we couldn't all fit in the country, which comprises only 0.17 square miles. I never had the good fortune to visit there, but if I was given the chance I would jump on it! It simply must be a most wonderful place!

There is no reason we couldn't at least try to emulate, as best we can, the Vatican City. I'm sure the Pope wouldn't mind. I know it would make me feel better.

We do have a very good country here, but we need to maintain its goodness and that is where the problem lies. Our goodness is eroding away like the sands on the beach. We need to work together to prevent all the good, Which is in this country, from being snatched right out from under us.

- - - - - - - - - - - - - - -

Assault on the American Flag!

We need to fight to keep our documents, the Declaration of Independence, the Constitution and the Pledge of Allegiance, their words and what they stand for, safe from being destroyed for no-good reason. We have a great thing going, don't let it slip away.

I think the biggest factor in making this nation great are its people and our documents help to keep us that way. I think we should use our Constitution as our countries standard, much like our ten commandments are our standard for discerning right from wrong. If you see violations in our constitution, you should start seeing those red flags again. If you don't know what is in our constitution, you should.

Our rights as Christians, as Roman Catholics in this country are based on what is written in our Constitution. The better you know our Constitution, the better you will be able to defend our rights. I know many of you already know these things, but obviously not all. It is clear these are things which need to be said simply by all the violations we already have, where no one does a thing. I speak mainly about our religious rights, but there are other violations.

This is the assault on the American flag I'm talking about. Some are outright violations and some are unsuccessful attempts. They haven't removed "One Nation, under God" yet, but they are constantly making attempts at it. Let your guard down and that could go away before you know what has happened. We need to draw a line and now is as good a time as any.

I do believe the majority of people in this great nation feel the same way I do, but they are afraid or at least

— — — — — — — — — —

hesitant in saying anything to anyone. Afraid of being politically incorrect or of being called a racist. This is why I say you need to know the documents such as the Constitution well and arm yourself with knowledge and back up your arguments. You don't need to be a constitutional scholar. You just need to know the basics.

We are letting things get way out of hand. The longer we wait, the longer it will take and the harder it will be to make any fixes. We shouldn't have to do any of this. I can certainly think of better things to do. There is only one problem. If we don't do anything who will?

If our soldiers and sailors can give their lives for us, the least we could do is to make sure they come back to the same country they left! With the same Constitution, the same Declaration of Independence and the same Pledge of Allegiance. We don't have to give our lives like they do. We only need to make sure the people we put into office treats these powerful documents with respect or you pull your vote for them and give it to someone who will.

The next question is, "How can you know how our representatives will vote?" You need to question them or look at their past record. Go to some of their rallies and meetings. Yes, which means you must get out of the old easy chair and find out. If they are an incumbent, you could always check their past voting record, which usually will give you a good clue as to how he or she would probably vote in the future. If you own a computer, you could probably get a lot of that sort of information right off of the internet. You may have to participate in things you have never done before, but don't you think it would be worth the trouble? It may not be all that bad anyway. It

- - - - - - - - - - - - -

could be a very interesting experience if you give it a try and you could learn a whole lot of things you may not have even counted on. Look at it as being a kind of adventure.

As I said previously, the voting booth is still the sure place to get results. Make sure your local politicians know us, as a group, are not going to stand for these things any longer. If we work together, we can make sure we hold on to the precious rights we have. I'm not just flapping my gums! I know you must see the same things I do. You also know it keeps getting worse year after year. You would have to be living in a cave not to see it!

Tune into the next section and see where else that pesky mold is infiltrating. We have let it go way too long! You will see what I'm talking about.

Chapter 3B

Not Our Money Too!

Yes, even our money! I'm sure you have heard and read the motto, "In God We Trust". The motto first appeared on our coins in 1864. That was one hundred and forty-six years ago, because of the many appeals of devout persons living throughout the country. This is part of our heritage! Does this mean we have no devout people around anymore? Can you believe this?

Why? Whom does this possibly hurt? This is ridiculous! I told you this mold is like a disease and it is showing up everywhere. It's not so much the money, it's the principle of the whole thing. It is like it is forbidden these days to mention God or Jesus in this country anymore. I don't know about you, but it gets me sick!

No, it hasn't happened yet, but look out! Turn your back for a moment and the dirty deed will be done. I'm totally disgusted with these things! I'm telling you it's everywhere and I think it is disgraceful. I hope you feel

— — — — — — — — — — —

the same and it isn't just the money, that's just an example. How about the Ten Commandments display, which had to be removed from an Arkansas courthouse! It was there for years. Have we had enough yet? Are we going to let them tear out our entire heritage? Enough is enough!

It is just one thing after another and if we don't put a stop to it we won't even know there are Christians in this country! We need to have some laws in this nation to preserve our great heritage.

I mean it! If we don't preserve our wonderful heritage, especially when it comes to religion, it will be lost forever. I really don't think this is what you want. I know we have atheists and agnostics in this country and they have their rights too, but this is our heritage we are talking about and what does it hurt? It is what our country was founded on. Simple facts, nothing more. It isn't like it is a hateful thing. We had slavery in the United States too, but you don't hear people banning books on the subject and that was a hateful thing! We are not banning books on slavery, because people need to know about slavery and why it was a very bad thing for this country. Unfortunately slavery is part of our heritage too, but we can look back now and learn many things from those mistakes.

Like it or not God was here right from the beginning, in more ways than one and it should be noted and even celebrated! Only Christians need or might want to celebrate that fact. Others could ignore it. It need not be forced on anyone. Certainly we would respect others feeling on the subject. What are we going to do if an individual says he or she is offended by the fruit apples?

- - - - - - - - - - - - -

Not Our Money Too!
— — — — — — — — — — — —

Are we going to ban them from this country so as not to offend anyone?

One other thing I would like to mention is the fact that Christians always seem to be the targets of these things as if it is a vendetta strictly on them. Another thing which gives me a bad taste in my mouth! It is like it is assault directly on us, which not only gets me upset, but scares me as to whom these predators of Christianity might be.

We go out of our way for other religions. I mean they are putting foot baths in some of our airports for the Muslims. I think that is being very hospitable to them and so be it. I would like to see a Christian try something like that, yeah right. That would be the day. The good old ACLU would be down their throats! If you read the papers or watch the news you know what I'm talking about. It raises a lot of suspicions in me of which I will let rest.

Like I first said about the money, it was fine for one hundred and forty-six years and now all of a sudden it's a problem? I detect more than simply what meets the eye going on. All I know is if we don't do something about it soon we will be sorry.

It shouldn't be a crime to observe the heritage and traditions of our country even if some of those customs are religious in nature. I have no problem with anyone practicing their faith or talking about their faith or even decorating in public view as per their faith within the law. However, I would expect the same respect for our faith, Roman Catholic or Christian, also within the law.   I believe we need laws to set some type of precedence for observing tradition or the heritage in our country. What I mean by that is when there has been a certain tradition

- - - - - - - - - - - - - -

developed and observed unfettered for a number of years it should have some protection. The protection I'm talking about would be the setting of a precedent if you will that would protect it from being stopped on the whim of anyone who happens to be irritated at the time.

This is the way I see it working. Lets say there is some proof or evidence of a certain ceremony, tradition or display occurring for a certain number of years and because it has occurred for this "particular" length of time it would set a precedent. Once the precedent has been set and in order for someone to have it discontinued or stopped they would have to get say a county, state or national referendum in their favor depending on the extent and type of event. The reason for the referendum would be to ensure there are a "majority" of people who wish for it to be stopped, not simply the whim of a few persons. You could use maybe ten years, twenty years, fifty years or whatever as a qualifier or a time necessary to set or constitute a legitimate precedent for a ceremony, tradition or display where a referendum would be required to remove it.

The reason I suggest this is to protect our honored events, ceremonies, traditions and matters of our heritage from just randomly being dissolved by just anyone for almost any reason. It would take a certain number of signatures on a petition to apply for a referendum call of a particular county, state or national area, of which the number of signatures necessary would also need to be determined. If the people involved got the required number of signatures, the referendum call would be invoked and placed on a ballet to be voted on by the general public for the area involved.

If you use a method such as this, it would take a "majority" of people to make any changes of events where precedents have been set. This means any changes made would be the decision of the majority rather than just a few individuals. It would provide some protection to these events unless the majority agrees they should be ended. In retrospect, I believe it would be a more equitable and fair way of handling events of this nature and making decisions to limit or discontinue them.

These events still could be eliminated through the referendum, but only by the voice of the majority. This is all I ask. I believe most of the traditions or ceremonies would continue, because I believe this would be what the "majority" would want. I could be wrong, but at least the majority would make the decision. It would be fair, because if the majority decides to eliminate a ceremony, tradition or some sort of public display they still could.

We shouldn't part with our time-honored traditions on the whim of a few should we? Some of these events have been going on since the birth of the nation! To just give them away without a fight doesn't seem right to me. The ceremonies and traditions I'm talking about aren't gross or pornographic. They are not disgusting public displays. Displaying the Ten Commandments at a courthouse for fifty years or more, disgusting, contemptible, come on! However, if it is that offensive to someone, get the required signatures, invoke a referendum vote and let the majority decide. Sounds fair to me. Personally, in this particular example I still think it would be wrong to remove the display, but at least it would be the decision of

— — — — — — — — — — —

a majority and disgusting to me, but fair. I will tell you a secret though. I have read articles about the place and if the referendum was the method used those Ten Commandments would still be there!

Now, my solution may not be perfect and someone very possibly could come up with a better method and I have no problem with that. I would say, go for it, whatever works! I hate to point out any kind of a dissent or discord on any current practices without offering up some type of alternative or solution along with it. I have always believed if you are going to criticize something you think is wrong, you should have some alternative or solution in your back pocket to bring to the table to correct it. I think a lot of times we are too eager to criticize something or someone without any suggestions or solutions to fix what your criticizing.

My solutions to problems, more often than not, may not be the best. I try to make my solutions something you could work from as a starting point, to hopefully aid in finding the best solution to a problem or an improvement to an existing procedure. Too often I hear people complaining or protesting things, but when you inquire as to what changes or improvements they suggest, they go silent.

I can only comment on the people around me, but by far the biggest percentage of them agree changes should be made to our current system. They don't like any more than I do the dismantling of our heritage bit by bit and would like, as I do, to see a stop put to it. At the same time no one I spoke to wants to offend anyone. They just think the way our decisions are made now are unfair to the majority.

- - - - - - - - - - - - - -

Not Our Money Too!
— — — — — — — — — — —

We have systems right now to preserve and protect our historic structures, national parks, forests, rivers and the extinction of our birds and animals. Don't we also need something to preserve and protect our heritage, founding and important documents, ceremonies and traditions? Take as an example, just one item, the Constitution, in that last sentence. If we don't preserve and protect, honor and respect our Constitution we could very easily lose everything else .....

Chapter 3C

School Children Excoriated!

The worst of the worst! Not even our schools are exempt from these outrages! Not even our schools! Can you hear what I say? Our schools seem to be another favorite place to attack us and our children. The mold has no shame, it is everywhere and growing.

It is one thing to go after adults, adults should be able to handle themselves, but when you go after the children you have crossed the line! While children are in school, they are still be molded by their parents, still being taught right from wrong, learning the difference between good and evil, learning how to properly conduct themselves, learning proper manners, learning respect and I can go on and on and on.

As Roman Catholics we have additional duties to teach our faith to our children so they can grow up to be fine Christian adults well versed in our religion and ready to

— — — — — — — — — — —

handle anything the world decides to throw at them, but that is when they have already grown into adulthood. When they are still children, the process of teaching and training is an ongoing experience. This could be a tough problem in today's schools.

I hear it all the time. It is almost approaching a daily circumstance or event. I hear a child in school getting suspended or expelled for praying during school hours, for drawing a crucifix in art class, for saying God in school, for writing a prayer in a study hall, for bringing a bible to school to read during lunch period, for praying on the high school football team before a game and I can go on and on and on.

Suspend or expel my child if he or she brings a knife or a gun to school, but not if he or she has a bible! What is happening with our schools? Is there no such thing as common sense anymore? You can't say a prayer in school? What law is that drawn from? I must be going crazy, or everyone else is crazy! I never dreamed in my life our schools would carry on like this. You can't write a prayer with the name's God or Jesus in it, pray to God, draw a picture of God, talk about God, have a book with God's or Jesus' name in it, it's all crazy! Outrageous! Sinful! Or the way I like to express it, a bunch of crap!

Don't give me that "separation of Church and state" crap either! It's a myth! That line does not exist in our Constitution! The intent of the Constitution was to ensure the government permitted freedom of religion or the freedom to have no religion and that the government didn't establish its own religion and require you to worship it. We should be tolerant of anyone who wants to

- - - - - - - - - - - - -

express their religion or at the same time anyone who wishes to be devoid of religion.

Tolerance, respect for everyone's beliefs and respect for their freedom of speech. We need to be tolerant of everyone's freedoms! Are we an intolerant society? All this commotion about religion in school could be avoided without government, without courts, without fighting, without yelling. Being Roman Catholic, doesn't mean shooting everyone who isn't! Sure we want everyone to join our faith, but not by force! They have to want to, to have it in their hearts. We will always be trying to convince people it is the right thing to do, but that would simply be exercising our freedom of speech for those who wish to listen.

I respect the rights of others to have different opinions and their religion as should be everyone. I don't get upset seeing others observe their religions as they wish, because I want to respect their rights and because I'm tolerant and expect to be treated likewise. I'm not going to take someone to court, because he is an atheist. He has a right to be an atheist if that is what he wants to be. All of this agitation in the schools is due to intolerance.

We need to be tolerant of each other and respect the rights of our fellow man. It's not all that difficult! A child in school should be able to pray as long as he or she doesn't force anyone else to or its not interrupting a scheduled class from its normal curriculum. Your child should be able to say "Merry Christmas" to someone without being carted off to prison. If your Jewish my child isn't going to punch you in the face for saying "Happy Hanukkah". Actually, what I would do, is return the greeting.

I think all of this would fall under the headings of common sense, tolerance and respect for others. There is no need to go beyond that. Now tolerance ends where violations of someone's rights begin. If I "force" you to say Jesus, if I "force" you to pray or if I "force" you to go to "my" Church or to any Church for that matter you would have a case. On the other hand, if you see me pray, will it kill you? If I ask you to pray with me, can't you just say I don't believe in prayer and be done with it? If I carry a bible will you start convulsing? If you see a picture of Jesus will you go insane? If children in the school play sing, Christmas carols, will all the Jewish children faint?

If you pray to Mecca, I assure you I won't call my lawyer. If you refuse to read a bible, I promise I won't slap you. If you don't want to say a prayer with the rest before a big high school football game, I won't want to have you expelled from school. If during the pledge of allegiance you don't want to say "under God" I won't have you flogged.

I hope we all see how ridiculous these arguments are when in print, in black and white. This is being intolerant of each other and at the same time ridiculous! As adults, can't we do any better than this? Does everything need to go to the courts these days? Do we really have to get lawyers involved, break out our dusty Constitutions? Some things I believe we can settle by being civilized human beings, by doing unto others as you wish done to you. Doesn't that sound familiar?

I have just broken the ice, there are many more examples exactly like this occurring all the time and it's

School Children Excoriated!

— — — — — — — — — — —

just not very cool. What does this teach our children? Is this the atmosphere we want in our schools? You need to remember our children are watching and learning from us all the time, especially when they are of school age.

Put yourself in the other person's shoes. Where could I have heard that before? Try to look through the other person's eyes. It's a good way to learn tolerance and to make the best of differing opinions. I think most of us would agree we want the best for everyone. If we continue on the route we are taking it will mean a lot of heartaches for everyone.

We have to remember freedom is for everyone, not just you or I. If I were an atheist and driving down the street and seen some Churches, should I be able to demand that they all be taken down, because Churches offend me? How preposterous would that be? At the same time, since I'm a Roman Catholic and believe all people in my sight should be baptized, should I be able to force you to get baptized? No, no, no, freedom doesn't work that way.

By now you must be saying all this is obvious. You know what? I wish you were right, then I wouldn't need to say, hear or see these things happening day after day. These all are very important things and they could all be solved in a very civilized way.

There is one thing that really does worry me. I believe there are a few, not many, but a few people who are intentionally causing these type problems. This is what really worries me the most. I think their intent is to cause havoc purposely. Some, because they want only their way of doing things and could care less about the freedoms of others and yet others who want to upset our entire system.

- - - - - - - - - - - - - -

School Children Excoriated!

These are the ones we have to be watchful of and stop. Some may even be politically orientated in their motives.

There are people among us who do not believe in our freedoms and will do anything to, piece by piece, have them removed or dismantle them. Guess where some of these culprits think is the best place to start? Correct, our schools! They feel if they form the children while they are young, they will be more susceptible to their ways when they get older.

We need to be on the watch for people of this nature. We need to make sure we teach our children at home and not to rely solely on the schools. The schools may have the best intent in mind, but there are a lot of things going on there. In your home you can make sure there are no distractions and not only make sure your children are aware of these things, but insure your children are properly taught no matter what.

It is very unfortunate we should have to even think about these things, but the world has no shortage of evil in it. We need to let our children know it too. Even the great United States of America has its share of evil and we need to deal with it, it is something we can't ignore or it will only get worse.

If the public school systems continue along this path and I was still raising my children, I would consider pulling them out of the public school system all together. We have fine Roman Catholic schools! There they not only learn the basics, reading, writing and arithmetic, but they also learn about their religion. They may cost you a little extra money, but well worth the expense.

There are other ways. You could put your children in

private schools other than religious ones. Some could put a real dent in your wallet though. They are not always feasible, because of the expense. You could even consider home schooling if you can devote the time to teaching your children on your own. Not anyone system is possible for everyone, but at least there are some alternatives if the public school system fails you.

If there is anywhere you want to protect the most, it has to be the school. Schools today are much more complicated than schools were years ago. These days you can't even let your child walk to school without fear they will be harmed in some way, shape or form. I don't envy anyone who has school age children these days. They have to be very careful of their children from the time they leave the home until they return back to the home.

We can make things much better concerning our schools by not making issues out of things which are totally unnecessary. I speak of the things I mentioned in the beginning of this section. Religion can be in the public school system as long as it isn't forced on anyone. We should be able to say things like merry Christmas, Jesus, happy Hanukkah, happy Easter and things of this nature. We should still be able to pray, reference a bible, any bible, sing songs of a religious nature no matter what that religion might be, to have prayers before that football game or just be able to speak of our religious beliefs. We should also be able to do none of the above if we don't want to. This is freedom of religion or freedom of no religion and was the intent of the Founding Fathers and the Constitution of our great United States.

Taking these things away in our schools is taking some

of our freedoms away no matter what you believe. All it takes is some tolerance. A lesson both adults and children could stand to learn in today's society, which is a mixture of many religions, cultures and peoples. We may all have different beliefs, but it shouldn't mean we can't live in harmony with each other and respect each other. I think that is why America is great and why we have so many people wanting to immigrate here.

Many people come here, because of our freedoms. Many of them don't enjoy the freedoms we have where they live. People come to the United States in multitudes for a reason. Lets try and keep it that way!

You may not like this, but thank God for our Constitution! Our Founding Fathers had it right from the beginning. Don't fix something that isn't broke! It got us through over two hundred years and that is an achievement in itself. It gives our children something to look forward to.

"One Nation, under God", music to my ears! It means freedom to me. Freedom of religion, freedom of speech, freedom, freedom, freedom! Without it us Roman Catholics could have a real big problem. Don't squander our freedoms away. Let them take one freedom away and then it will be another, then another and pretty soon we will have nothing. We need to stand fast and strong for the Constitution and above all the Ten Commandments, both for our children and ourselves.

It is time for us to get organized and fight to keep the freedoms we already have. We need to work at it and we need to work together. When you go to the ballot box let, your local and national officials know we together are going to vote for those officials who have respect for the sanctity of life, for our God given Commandments, for the maintenance and respect of our freedoms and our Constitution.

The battlefront is the voter's booth and if we get organized we will not only win the battle, but the war. As I said earlier, I know our religion and our Churches can't endorse any one person or political party and I wouldn't expect or suggest to them to do so. However, that does not mean you can't get the congregation together and list the essential points they should consider when they cast vote for prospective government representatives, whether they are incumbents or new candidates for political office. I will discuss those issues more in the next section and offer some suggestions as to how this might be accomplished.

Chapter 4

The Voter's Booth.

Our secret weapon, our vote! If you are serious about getting this country on the right track again, you need to be thinking about the voter's booth. You need to understand the clergy and our churches may not endorse any one candidate or political party. Those are the rules. This does not mean we can't discuss what we are looking for in our elected officials to promote God's laws and to allow us to freely express and practice our religion.

My message here is not to break the rules. We need to respect the laws of this nation or we end up with chaos. Roman Catholics have certain duties and obligations as you well know. When you vote, you should be voting and electing officials for the betterment of our society in the United States. This means voting for officials who will respect God' laws and will not choke off our freedoms to engage in the practice and expression of our religion. Right now I don't see that happening. What I do see occurring is a great allegiance to the political parties on behalf of our members.

I know you want to respect your parents and that is a good thing. When I ask people how they might vote I hear the same thing almost all of the time. They tell me my parents voted Democratic and my grandparents voted Democratic, so I will vote Democratic too. Now, their answer could have just as well had been Republican or Independent. The vote tends to become a tradition in a lot of families.

I can understand a person respecting their parents decisions when they placed their votes, but voting for a particular party or even for a particular candidate, should be "your" decision, not theirs. Your parents may have voted Republican or Democratic or whatever years ago and it may very well have been the correct decision to make at the time or back at that time the candidate they chose may have been the best candidate to put into office. Times are constantly changing and so are the candidates and their parties and you need to adjust likewise.

What is the purpose of your vote? Shouldn't it be to elect an official who will have a platform which would be the best for the country and the best for maintaining God's laws and our religious freedoms before anything else? I would hope you would answer yes to that last question. Those might not be all the reasons, but should be the bare minimum of reasons. You should never vote blindly! You shouldn't be voting for a political party solely for its name, but for its candidate and what that candidate stands for.

- - - - - - - - - - - - - - -

The Voter's Booth.
— — — — — — — — — —

This is not a contest between the Democrats and the Independents or the Republicans and the Democrats, it's for establishing a country with human rights and freedoms and maintaining the constitution. If there are any losers here, it won't be the Republicans, Democrats or the Independents, but the people! We are "all" Americans! There should be only one real difference in any of the parties and that is how we get to our goals in respecting human rights, freedom of religion and speech or, as stated in the Declaration of Independence, " ..... all men are created equal, that they are endowed by their Creator with certain unalienable Rights, that among these are Life, Liberty and the pursuit of Happiness ....."

We are voting "for" each other, not "against" each other. This is not a football game! All our goals should be basically the same. We may not agree on how to achieve those goals, but once our officials are elected we should all support them as a united country so they can do the work they have been elected to do. However, if they go off track, for example with abortion (a clear violation of God's law), we need to step in and get them back on track. Amen to that .....

Voting blindly is voting a certain way, because everyone else does, because your parents do, because all your friends are, because he or she is a Democrat or because he or she is a Republican. You should be voting for what the candidate's stands for, for his or her positions on certain issues such as abortion or euthanasia or stem cell research or freedom of speech or other important factors.

You should not be voting for a person because he or

- - - - - - - - - - - - -

she looks presidential! Looks presidential! Are you kidding me? What kind of a reason is this? You may laugh, but I hear it all the time. You vote for what the candidate stands for, not for what the candidate looks like. This is not a beauty contest!

What you need to do is to find out what the candidate stands for, his or her position on important issues, for issues of faith, your freedoms and your country. I'm afraid this is not happening, but should be.

Many times I ask people about their politics and whom they might be voting for in an upcoming election. They give me their answer and then I ask them why they are picking that particular candidate and I almost get the same type of responses every time. Usually the first answer is I don't know and they don't! Why even vote? If that isn't their answer, sometimes it's because everyone is. Once in a while I get something like he has such beautiful blue eyes. There is always someone who will say how he just seems to be a nice guy. You know, some really good reasons to vote for a candidate. Yeah right! There is also the I always vote Independent or I always vote Democrat. I always follow that answer by asking them why they do that and I usually always get the same answer. I don't know and they don't!

Forget asking anyone what their candidate's platform is. If you do that, you most probably will first have to explain what a platform is and if you need to do that you already know you have a prize winner here! Even if they understand what a platform is don't expect them to know what their candidate's is, because there is nine out of ten chances they will have no clue!

The Voter's Booth.

— — — — — — — — — — —

My object here is not to be a wise guy, but what I said is true, I know I have tried it. All you are seeing are my results. We have some serious problems in this country when it comes to voting. I can only divulge what information I have received amidst those I have personally had come in contact with to offer as my sampling. It doesn't look very promising if the whole country is this way. We need to get a lot more serious about our voting or we are going to lose everything. I'm quite sure this is why we are in the predicament we are in now.

Just educating ourselves on our choices would be a big improvement. The absolute minimum would be at least to find out what the platforms of the candidates are before even considering voting. How can you possibly cast an intelligent vote if you don't even know your candidate's positions on the critical issues for the office he or she is running for?

If you want to make the correct and informed choice, you need to find these things out. I know the next question, "How does one know these things?" First, you need to be up on current affairs. You need to watch the news or read the newspapers. You don't need to make it a twenty four hours a day thing, but at least be aware of the main issues out there, when you do vote. It's critical to your religion, your family and to your country. Another thing, don't believe everything you hear! Guess what? Candidates for office have this bad habit of saying any and everything they think you want to hear just to get into office. If you like the color blue, so do they. If you agree with the pro-life movement, so do they. This all sounds good until they get into office and then proceed to do

- - - - - - - - - - - - - -

anything they like, which can be the total opposite of what they have told you!

All right, this tends to make things a bit more difficult. If you can't trust a politician to tell you the truth what can you do? Well, if he or she is an incumbent, has held office before, you can check their past voting history. In other words, pay attention to what they say, but most importantly what they do or what they have already done. Their past record says a lot and probably says it better than they would!

If they are new candidates it is much tougher, because you don't have a past record to rely on. In a case like this you could go on their backgrounds and past history in other professions they have held and their moral lifestyle and opinions and hope for the best if they are your choice. The main thing would be to find out about as much of their past as you possibly can.

I must stress this has to be done. You need to investigate their past history and their platforms to make a good and informed decision. If you don't do at least that much, it would compare to the politicians who vote on a bill without reading it. Crazy! You might even attend some political events like a town hall meeting to hear what they have to say in person and maybe ask them some questions face to face.

If you are like me and if it was up to me I could do without politics, but some things are necessary evils. I know there are many things I would rather do than be following politics, but if you don't, things like abortions get put into law. This makes politics a necessity to keep our nation on track for us, our children and their children.

- - - - - - - - - - - - -

The Voter's Booth.

— — — — — — — — — — —

We have to do other things before voting. We have to figure out what we stand for, the things we will tolerate and those things which we won't. This is where we have to come together and meet and put our needs, beliefs and goals on the table. If you get organized and figure out what is and isn't acceptable for a candidate position your choice should be easy. This can be done by getting a Church group organized and forming a list of unacceptable principles, morals and values, such as pro-choice or stem cell research, which would be cause to drop any candidate from consideration when determining whom you will be voting for.

The list I speak of is a very critical item and should not be taken lightly. Get it on paper and make sure everyone knows the most important factors and why they're important. Not a candidate's name need be mentioned! This list would contain our beliefs and what we should be looking for in a candidate when voting. It would render some candidates ineligible for consideration regardless of their party affiliation.

The list would have one other very important element. This may be the most important element! You need to make sure everyone knows their candidate's platform or position with respect to every item on the list. If you don't know, you need to find out, because you shouldn't be voting for that candidate until you do find out. If the candidate is unclear about his or her position for any item on the list, they should be eliminated from the eligible list!

The list is important! If a particular candidate is not forthright with their position for any of our items contained on our list, they should not be trusted to do what

- - - - - - - - - - - - - -

is right on our behalf. Our list would contain the very "minimum" basic beliefs we deem acceptable in a candidate. If your candidate can't even espouse that much, he or she isn't acceptable and we need to look for someone else who can!

The list would require us to do our homework. If we have preference for a certain candidate we need first to find out if they meet the "minimum" requirements as noted on our list. In today's age we can probably do that by going to the candidate's web site if they have one. I suspect nowadays most do. If not, you can check their past history in office if there is one or simply call them and ask. Now this may seem a bit difficult, but actually most of the items on the list you may be able to check off right away, because some candidates make their positions obvious and are even very passionate about certain points. Some candidates may be running on a major point in the list such as being passionately against pro-choice or abortion, which would be my kind of candidate!

Our lists need not be the "only" criteria for selecting a candidate, but a major and necessary factor in determining their eligibility for consideration. I also like to look at their moral behavior if known, because it should give you a good idea of your candidate's ethics, standards, values and ideals. If they are all good, you have a real winner. However, if your candidate is always being caught up in lies and is always in the news for disrespecting their spouse you may want to reconsider your choice. Good moral, ethical and honorable behavior makes a candidate an exceptional candidate rather than an average or below an average candidate.   Putting these Church groups together would be essential in ensuring everyone is on the same page and everyone understands what is on the list, why and their importance. This has got to be a joint effort so we can utilize the full force of our numbers to correct bad laws. Bad laws would be any of man's laws violating God's laws such as abortion, euthanasia, etc., etc. It would or could also ensure no new wrongs are instituted into law.

Our Church groups could meet at our Church halls or meeting rooms, maybe at various Church members houses or even on-line at your computer. Since everyone already meets at Church for mass it would probably make the Church halls or meeting rooms the best logical place to hold the meetings, but whatever works best for everyone. In my opinion it would be most effective to meet in person and see and hear face to face what needs to go on the list and which items would have the greatest priorities and make obvious the most passionate issues. It would also be crucial to get all the Churches in your immediate area involved so you can form an entire network of Churches with the same list. Our churches communicate with each other regularly anyway, so it shouldn't be too difficult to have representatives from all the Churches in the area meet and compare notes. If nothing else they could make some telephone calls to insure, everyone is following the same game plan. The more Churches we get together in our various areas, the more powerful our votes will become for all the elections, local, state or national.

I contend for this first crusade "abortion" should be placed at the top of our list. Crusade #1, the abolition of abortion, which is to me the most pressing and serious order of business. Pro-Life should also be marked as a requirement in any candidate's platform. In other words, if pro-life isn't a priority on the candidate's platform he or she should be dropped from the list of eligible candidates. This is why I say you need to know the candidate's platform, so you can make that decision.

Again, the reason I think the abortion issue should top the list is because of its importance. Remember, every minute of every day our unborn babies are being aborted. Literally millions of unborn babies every year are being slaughtered and the sooner it's stopped the better. This fact alone gives it the highest of priorities and allows for no wasted time in getting the job done.

Personally, if there are no candidates in the election who are pro-life I will not vote for that office! Period! I will not ever, ever pull the lever for a pro-choice candidate! I couldn't live with myself if I did! No, I'm not perfect, I make my share of mistakes and I'm a sinner like everyone else, but I "do" know better than to vote pro-choice! If I don't get anything right, this will be the one thing I do get right. I don't believe in legalized murder and never will! If that sounds cruel, think of the unborn baby and then try to tell me I'm wrong. I should not even have to say this. Above all and considering everything, I know in my heart, in my soul, I'm right and it is the right way to be. Generally speaking, as a rule, I try to have an open mind for everything I do, but there are exceptions to all rules and this is "my" exception!

We are so into our children in the United States. We even have many corporations using babies in their advertising to promote their products and services. You always see advertising and public announcements promoting our children's safety and their proper handling and training. Our talk shows are often geared to raising our children in the proper environment and giving them appropriate loving and care. After all that and in the end we have thousands and thousands of unborn babies being aborted every year! Hypocrites! What else would you call it? Hypocrites! Unbelievable, yet oh so true, disgusting and sick.

We give more respect to our pets than we do to our babies! Where are our priorities? Don't get me wrong I love animals. You can't beat a good cat or dog as a pet. All animals hold a special place in my heart and I wouldn't think of purposely hurting any of them, domestic or not.

When I say "priorities" with respect to our animals, I need to explain the circumstances on a particular day when I was listening to the news on the radio. I heard a report about a car wash business. Evidently there was a small stream, which ran right next to it and the owners managed to acquire around thirty ducks, which they somehow got to make that part of the stream their home. The ducks just made the chore of washing your car a little bit more of an enjoyable experience. Well, someone got mad at the management for some reason and purposely killed all the ducks in the area for revenge. They reported on the radio the duck killers could get as much as eight years in prison for their crime if caught. I continued listening to the news and soon thereafter there was a report of a person who "raped" a three-year-old girl. He had already been caught, went to court and was sentenced to four months in prison. What is wrong with this picture?

- - - - - - - - - - - - - -

The Voter's Booth.

— — — — — — — — — — —

Please understand I have nothing against ducks. In fact, many times I have gone to the park with a loaf or two of bread solely to use to feed the ducks at the park and enjoy their beauty. Eight years for killing ducks and four months for raping a three-year-old child just doesn't sound right to me. I definitely think the duck killers should do some time for their crime, but what kinds of value are we putting on our children in comparison? This is just one example. I can give you many more. Again, in my heart I know there is something wrong here. I'm not sure, what to do about it, but I'm confident there is something here, which needs to be addressed and fixed.

There are times I hear of animal abuse, such as dog fights, killings or beatings and the like and people seem to come out of the woodwork to help stop or prevent these things and see the people involved are taken to court to pay for their actions. I like that. It's a very good way to be. Abuses like that are uncalled for and need to be stopped. At the same time, someone has an abortion, kills their child and not a word is said. What is wrong with this picture? Do I need to give a lesson on moral values, the sanctity of life? Do we have more respect for the animal kingdom than our own human race? Again, I love animals, but there is something very wrong in this country when we will jump to save a dog from a beating, but we won't lift a finger to help an unborn child from being murdered! I know that must sound awful and it should!

Like I said previously the Church and clergy can't tell you who to vote for or what political party. All that really needs to happen when your Church group gets together is to make a list of what can't be tolerated on a candidate platform and what should be on their platform. Once you have the list you can take it home and compare it to the platforms of all the candidates who are running for office. Here is where you can weed out any and all "unacceptable" candidates and make your choice from whatever candidates remain. You still have your choice of those candidates, which you haven't eliminated and which you have already determined are acceptable through use of your list.

You're not breaking the law you are simply voting with respect to your religious beliefs. You also have the satisfaction of knowing you are doing the right things for everyone concerned. This won't change the laws overnight, but it will in time. Candidates will see we are serious in our beliefs and that we won't tolerate any violation of God's law or of our religious freedoms or any of our freedoms for that matter.

We must get together for all elections, local, state and national. This is not going to be a one time deal. One vote will not change all the laws, which need changing. We need to do this on a regular basis until the job is done. When will that be? When we can say, abortion is no longer legal in the United States! Our goal to abolish abortion will be complete. Crusade #1 is over and a success! In the mean time, we can be saying those things, which need to be said to those who are in need of being educated in the importance and value of life even of the unborn. Those who are contemplating abortion need to hear why life is sacred, a blessing and a gift to us all. They need to know and hear a new life begins at conception and are our treasures and miracles given to their parents from

The Voter's Booth.

— — — — — — — — — — —

God.

If we can make our new mothers understand the sanctity of life, we can make the law irrelevant. They won't want to seek an abortion and until the law changes that is exactly what we must do.

We must change the law no matter what. We can do it, but we have to persevere, because it will take time and many votes. In the interim we have to break our silence and let our children know abortion is an unacceptable act. I fear many times abortion has occurred simply because no one took the time to sit down and explain why it is wrong, why man's law doesn't make it right and the consequences that encompass such a decision.

At this stage you might be thinking you could make your own list as I indicated without the Church group and determine unacceptable candidates without ever leaving the house. While this may be true, it won't be very effective in changing the laws. You see what we need is the Church group. We need to spread the word and get the word out to everyone. Yes, you could do it all on your own, but our power is going to be in our numbers. We need to get everyone involved or it won't work and things will go on as they were. You can't have a crusade of one, you don't need weapons, but you do need an army!

Our priests obviously would be our best source for helping us to construct this list and determining our priorities. They can't tell us who to vote for or what party to vote for, but they can tell us what is important to our religion and help us to make our decisions based on truth, righteousness and respect for God's laws. The names of the candidates involved for a particular election need

- - - - - - - - - - - - - -

— — — — — — — — — — —

never even be mentioned. Ultimately we have to make our own decisions when voting. Sometimes the decisions can be real tough, but with guidance from our newly formed Church groups and our priests, that decision could be better for us all and much easier to make.

What we have so far in our crusade is the forming of our new Church group, the developing of a network between our Church and the other Churches in the area and construction of our list to help in determining what would be an acceptable or unacceptable candidate for whomever that candidate might be. As you see it will take some work to get everyone together on this, but it will be well worth the time. We are not quite done yet. We now need to ensure as many of our members as possible get involved. If no one shows up at the meetings, nothing will get accomplished.

I did indicate before we should have face to face meetings to be the most effective and I still believe that to be true. I also think we should develop alternatives for those who might not be able to make a meeting or meetings. It is tough enough to get people to attend mass regularly much less to go to these meetings.

I do have some alternatives to aid in getting our people together. One possibility I came up with is to have a meal and refreshments served or available for the attendees to help in making the experience more enjoyable and more enticing for better attendance. As serious as the meetings will be, it doesn't mean it has to be a bad or a boring experience, we can make it enjoyable and fun and still get what we need accomplished. We can also take a list of e-mail addresses of our members and e-mail notes about the

- - - - - - - - - - - - - -

meeting and even send them the list we construct and any other pertinent information, such as voting days and times and even possible transportation opportunities for those who might not be able to make it to the polls on their own. We could even construct a simple web site where our members could go to and get information, meeting times and dates.

I think one of the biggest factors we will have to deal with is time. We have such busy lives today. It isn't going to be easy to get people together to accomplish our goals. I think one thing in our favor is it shouldn't be too hard and take too long to construct our lists, so we shouldn't need to schedule that many meetings. I think realistically if you look ahead to the elections times and if you schedule, say a meeting, once a month for three months prior to an election you should be able to easily accomplish what is necessary to get the work done for that particular election. After that you schedule, when necessary, for any proceeding elections and just make it an ongoing thing. Eventually our Church members will get used to the routine and after the first or second elections any rough edges will smooth out and you will have regular system installed for all future elections.

What is good about this whole new system is the fact that with the great number of Christians we have in this country we should be able to eventually fix many and hopefully all our concerns with our present laws. Not only that, but we will have a system to ensure we never get into a predicament like this again and maintain some sanity in this great country of ours.

Lets face it we need to do something. We can't let

things keep on going as they are. There are lives at stake, many lives. This isn't just for us, but for our children and their children and so on. This will also teach our children what they can do when it becomes their turn for their generation. It will also show them we are ready to fight evil when it shows its face.

I don't like to point out problems unless I have solutions to them or at least some alternatives. What I have just explained is a possible solution and it's "my" solution. I truly think it would work if we do it as I explained. This is not to say I'm not open to any other alternatives. I'm no expert in this area by any means. My solution doesn't need to be the only possible solution or the solution at all. If there are better ways of running this crusade so be it. I would be thrilled to hear any other and better methods to accomplish the task. We are all in this together and any constructive input would be greatly welcomed! We are a family of one, all brothers and sisters, striving for the same goals. If there are any budding geniuses out there whom, have fantastic ideas or solutions to this problem, step forward and be counted! There will be no objections I assure you.

We can't be, all talk and no action! We actually have to get out of our recliners and do something. We got in this mess by our deference, complacency and lack of the insight needed to take action in preventing these abominations from coming to pass in the first place.

Many times we are content with doing the right moral and righteous things for ourselves. Teaching and showing our families and relatives what we need to do, to be good Roman Catholics and Christians and how to properly interact with our friends and neighbors who surround us. If we do this, we can grow great families and neighborhoods for us all. I'm all for that. It is the way it should be everywhere! Unfortunately, it isn't like that everywhere, so some of us, as good as we are and as good as we do, need to broaden our horizons.

We have to extend our reach beyond our immediate surroundings and families. Your block in the neighborhood may be fantastic and everything may be wonderful, but if all the other blocks in your neighborhood are in dire need of direction and of the Christian ways you still can have many problems. Remember, your family doesn't stay in the house twenty four hours. They have to eventually go out into the neighborhood and into the world, so if there are problems out there we have to work on them too. Keep in mind, if your block is doing great its not a bad thing, but what I am saying is it may not be good enough.

One bad block in the middle of ten great blocks can cause problems for everyone. One of the ways we can help to make sure everyone's block is on the right track is to make sure, at a minimum, the laws governing them are in line with God's laws or commandments. The whole purpose here is to see that, that happens. What we need to look out for is everyone in our neighborhoods, towns, cities, states and ultimately our nation.

God gave us a fantastic gift, the Ten Commandments! They help to make us a civilized and wonderful society to boast of his greater glory. We need to make sure man's laws don't interfere with God's laws and only complements them. If we do that, we will have the greatest nation on earth!

Break the silence and do something. Make Crusade #1, the abolition of abortion, our first "winning" battle and save the lives of millions of unborn children in this great nation of ours. If you would like to give your life some real meaning, I couldn't think of a better way to start!

Part II
My Peeves &
Two Cents Worth

Chapter 5

The Year 2012 - Here We Go Again!

I have to laugh. Sorry! Here we go again. Ever since the beginning of time, well, at least from as far back as I can remember, which is close, the world was coming to an end. I'm fifty-five now and when I was a little kid, maybe seven or eight, I could remember running home and telling my mother, the world was going to end soon! I heard someone, an adult, talking about it. She had to laugh too! Evidently it wasn't the first time she had ever heard about the earth coming to an end.

It never fails, every few years we go through this. It's really amazing, but I'm still here! The world hasn't ended yet. What happened? Right now we are doing the 2012 thing and when that is over, they will find some other reason and some other date.

Not all that long ago it was the year 2000, the new millennium. All the computers in the world were going

- - - - - - - - - - - - - - -

to blow up and everyone would die! Well, something like that. Nope, still here. I have really managed to live through many world endings. I imagine I really shouldn't make light of these things, because some people really take these things serious. However, it is hard to be serious, when you have already lived through so many of these apocalyptic events. Everything from computers to the way the planets were lining up at the time could cause these events to take place.

I do have an excellent solution to the problem of the world ending with all of its doom and gloom, but I will share that with you in time. First, for those who don't already know, this event, the world ending event, occurs routinely. I want you to know, this isn't the first time and probably, hopefully, it won't be the last. I have lived through many of these events and I'm pretty sure you will too. If not, oops.

Lets talk about 2012. I guess, because it's the next major event coming up, we should get this one out of the way first, so we will be more prepared for the "next event". I would greatly appreciate it if you would really think hard about the last statement I made.

As I understand it, this calender date, 2012, came about through some intense calculations from an ancient civilization. As you all know, when you are making intense and extensive calculations, there is always room for error. I bring this up for a reason. If there is an error it could really give way to some horrible situations and circumstances.

Even a small error in calculations could be devastating! Lets say they are only one year off. Maybe the year is really 2011. Oops! It seems to be we would be caught a bit off guard. Not a very good thing in this case! We get ourselves all prepared for 2012 and boom in 2011 it is all over and done. They would have been only one year off, but wow what an impact that error would make! I hope my scenario doesn't make you have that uneasy feeling inside.

No one says they would have to be off one year too late. What if they were off one year the other way, you know, the actual year was 2013. I think this would yield pretty bad results also. You see, you would be waiting the whole year, the year 2012 and nothing would happen. What would you do then? You would just laugh it off as another world ending gone sour and let out a real big sigh of relief, because nothing happened. Then, low and behold, 2013 comes around and boom! Oops! I know, this scenario isn't much better.

This is all assuming they made an ever so little mistake and were only one year off. Who knows, maybe they made a bigger mistake or maybe they were wrong all together or maybe our interpretation was totally incorrect?

Either way you look at it, it doesn't sound very good. The way I look at it, is these people have too much time on their hands and need to find better things to do. As a people, we have such a fascination with the world coming to an end it gets to the point of being ridiculous.

Yes, I have read the book of Revelation in the Holy Bible and I do believe it with all my heart and soul! I also believe the end of the world could come at any time. I believe it will be a most horrible event and I hope I am already gone before it really happens, long gone! Many people believe the same, because they believe in the bible, but many of those people forget one very important thing. This thing I speak of is also in the Holy Bible and I believe this too.

Matthew 24:36

"But of that day and hour no one knows, neither the angels of heaven, nor the Son, but the Father alone."

These are the words of the Lord Jesus Himself. If you are going to be consistent and believe in the Holy Bible, you have to believe everything. I believe this line is also true and we are fooling ourselves if any of us think we are going to figure out when that time comes, the end of our earth as we now know it, that is.

I can understand the interest in knowing when this all important time comes. It would be only natural for anyone to be concerned. I myself have engaged in some intense scrutiny coupled with a heightened measure of contemplation and deep consideration in regards to this particular event. In doing so, I have come to the conclusion we are all devoid in our concerns and our efforts are at best misguided when considering the factors which bear the most importance or significance in this affair.

What is really important is not the date, but our preparation for the date. I have the solution! I spoke of this solution near the beginning of this section and I will reveal what I personally think is the way you should concentrate your efforts in getting beyond this. These are my personal thoughts on the subject and I believe they might be helpful to you.

If it should really happen and the end is in sight, what do you think you should do? What do you think you can do? Do you think you can stop this from occurring? A most thought-provoking dilemma isn't it?

I know what I would do and you might want to bend your ears to listen for a moment. It will only take a moment for my solution is very simple. I will also make a one hundred per cent guarantee it will work! Once you know the solution you won't even have to give this any more thought. I'm confident, because "I believe". I'm confident, because I'm a Roman Catholic who has been armed with weapons for just this type of situation and the weapons come from the Lord himself!

This is the plan: If you even just slightly suspect, the apocalypse is near what you need to do is to find a confessional and a priest. Once you have found them give the best confession to the priest you could have ever possibly imagined giving, given right straight from the heart, then attend Mass and receive communion. Once you have completed this, you pray and continue praying until everything has past. Done! That is it! The problem is solved! One hundred per cent effective! You can thank me in heaven, when you get there and I most humbly will acknowledge and embrace your gratefulness. I know I will be there, because I resolve to do the same.

What you need to understand is, it's your soul, not your body, that is the key or important factor. I sleep well at night, because I believe. My most important and only main concern in my life, is my soul, to make my soul as clean as I can possibly get it. This, of course, is in regards to me personally. I don't want to sound or be self-centered, I would also want to insure my family, relatives and friends do the same. If I do that I know everyone will be a winner in the end, no matter what.

Remember, our great Lord gave us the power to handle any and everything, we just have to put to use the wonderful gifts he has given us. Think out of the box! The Lord gave us the tools, we just need to put them to use.

Even if time is of the essence, but only then, you can handle it. In this case you would still need to find a priest and have him give you absolution. However, he would only be able to do that when there is no time to do anything else.

Of course, if you keep tabs on your soul and keep it as clean as possible always, you need not do a thing, but pray! I believe our priests would prefer this to all other methods available and rightly so.

If you truly believe, which I hope you do, you have nothing to worry about ever! If you don't believe, you have a real problem and need to get it fixed and in a hurry, because you never know what is waiting around the corner from you. The earth is only your pit stop to heaven and your main concern should be to keep your soul clean. That is, free from sin, especially mortal sin.

These doomsday patriots I find are more concerned about their bodies, then their souls. It should be the other way around. If you are a Roman Catholic you should already know this, but I do want to say the things that should be said, but seem never to get said. I feel many of the people in our own religion get swept up in the details of these things and forget their basics. They don't see the forest for the trees tend to get in the way. I don't profess to be another Einstein by any means, just trying to get all my brothers and sisters on the right path by reiterating the basics which I have witnessed many have forgotten.

Learn to use the weapons and the tools the Lord has given you and you will all sleep much better. I know I do and I'm still learning. Being an ex-college professor I love learning and the more I learn, the more I realize I don't know. Also, the more I learn about my beautiful Roman Catholic religion, the more I love it. I have much more to learn and I can't wait to learn it!

Unfortunately I got a late start in learning the Roman Catholic religion. The fault is all mine, but true. You see, I always had this fascination with learning things and I quickly found out you need to read to learn. Even Einstein and the genius he was, wasn't born with all his knowledge. I suspect he had to do plenty of reading to get to the apex of his knowledge. So, while everyone was reading their novels, I was reading textbooks. I felt if I have to read, let it be a book that will teach me something, anything, things that I like. I have since changed my attitude and now I read many genres of books and even some novels, depending on my mood at the time.

I was consumed with reading books in my profession, which was electrical engineering and marveling at the amazing achievements of man in this field. I did this for many years and managed to gain much knowledge in the field with much more yet to learn.

I stayed away from the Holy Bible! I always managed to get the King James version of the Holy Bible and it would always make my head spin! The English written in this Bible was way too foreign to me! I never could seem to get through more than about three verses and my head would be going in circles and I would give up. I would read the three verses and say, "What?" They call this English? Not where I come from! So, I did that rationalizing thing and said to myself, "Ah the Bible is about God and God is great and does wonderful things, what else do you need to know?" With that, I put the Bible aside and went on to the wonderful and amazing books of man and man's knowledge.

Well, one day I was sitting at the dinner table with my best friend in the whole wide world Kimberly and I told her my view of the Bible. She had most kindly invited me to dinner at her house and what she said next changed my whole life! She asked me, "Did you ever try reading a Roman Catholic Bible?" What! You mean to tell me there is a Roman Catholic bible! I thought a Bible was a Bible, was a Bible. Wrong, wrong and wrong again.

This changed everything! I went on-line and investigated the notion of a Roman Catholic Bible. I don't know where I have been or what I have done, but no one, but no one ever even suggested to me there was a different type of Bible. Maybe I was too obsessed in man's creations to even notice. Since then I have found out that the New American Bible was the choice of the Roman Catholic church for the reading in Mass, so I promptly purchased one. To my delight found out it was written in English, I mean "real" English, you know the kind you speak at the dinner table English! I could actually read more than three verses now and understand what was written! What a revelation! Quite a discovery for me. I said that Kimberly gal is pretty cool! She really enlightened me and I thank her for that.

Ok, so now I will read the Roman Catholic Bible. I loved it, so well paraphrased! I really give my compliments to the Church, they have a winner. Anyone could understand even some of the most difficult verses. I quickly noticed the Old Testament was much larger than the New Testament, so I decided to read about three chapters in the Old Testament, to every one of the chapters in the New Testament. This way I could learn from each and complete them in about the same amount of time.

I started with Genesis in the old Testament and with the Gospel of Matthew in the New Testament. Well, let me tell you what, The Gospel of Matthew just blew me away! I immediately found out I was right, the Bible was exactly what I had thought, with one **"BIG"** exception, there was much, much, much, much more!

The Gospel of Matthew totally amazed me in so many ways! I couldn't believe it, figuratively speaking. All the Gospels are fantastic, but the Gospel of Matthew just happened to be the first Gospel I read and oh what a book! Amazing!

Guess what was one of the most amazing things I realized about the Bible. Forget it, you will never guess. It was a book of wisdom! Let me explain please. This is I and I alone, but the way I envision the Bible now is probably unique to me, but maybe not. I say that, because of the way the Bible was introduced to me, so late in life I mean.

I was always amazed at the great knowledge man has achieved through his existence and I maintain that same feeling, but now I look at man's knowledge as just "plain" knowledge and the knowledge you get from the Bible, a "special" kind of knowledge, as "wisdom" from the Lord, well above, above and above the knowledge of man.

I spent much of my life studying some of the most difficult texts of knowledge from man. Feeling really good about myself when I got through them and understood them. Man has really gone far in a reasonably short amount of time. What I realized when I read the Bible, is that this book far exceeds anything man has written. It was very obvious to me right away. I don't want to take anything away from man's knowledge, but there is no comparison with the wisdom you find in the Holy Bible. There is no contest!

Attaining knowledge is one thing, but realizing wisdom from the Holy Bible completely overshadows any knowledge man has to offer. Man's knowledge is great, but wisdom from the Holy Bible has no bounds. Henceforth, my whole universe was turned on its head when I discovered just some of the wisdom contained in the most wonderful book in the world, the Holy Bible.

I know I have gone on quite a tangent here, but for those who may still be in the dark as I was I feel it is something I had to get off of my chest. As much as I love the Roman Catholic faith I feel they need to do more to encourage their congregations to read the Bible and in the United States, particularly, the New American Bible for easier understanding. Its still based on the King James Bible, but written in the common English we use today in the United States. This way you can spend your time soaking up the wisdom, which is contained in the Bible rather than spending most of your time trying to interpret what it is saying.

I thank the Roman Catholic Church for making the Holy Bible accessible to me in "real" English, where before it was not. My only regret is that I didn't find this out sooner in my life. It has given me the ability to find solutions to problems, such as the year 2012. It also reminds me, that no matter what, the Lord is right here, right now, beside me and no matter what happens we "together" can get through it, even the year 2012! I know now I'm never alone and either are you. The last sentence, when you really believe it and really understand it makes all the difference in the world! This is just one little piece of wisdom you can derive from the Holy Bible which can change your life forever.

It took me a long time to figure that out, I do have quite a thick skull. I sincerely hope it doesn't take you as long, wisdom is a most wonderful thing to possess even in the tiniest amount, better than all the gold and silver on earth. Make it a goal to enrich your life with the wisdom of the Holy Bible and you will amaze yourself and make your life much more enjoyable in so many ways. I know, because I already have. It has been nothing less than a very fantastic experience and an ongoing experience. Once you start, it seems as though you can't get enough. No regrets here!

Revelation 22:7

*"Behold, I am coming soon," Blessed is the one who
keeps the prophetic message of this book.*

- - - - - - - - - - - - - -

The Year 2012 - Here We Go Again!
— — — — — — — — — — —

Ask anyone I work with, I'm almost always in a very good mood and happy. I would say about ninety-nine per cent of the time. They would tell you. Do you know why? The Bible and prayer give you piece of mind. That's it! This piece of mind I speak of is a really good thing to possess and for the biggest part of my life I didn't have it. Then came the Bible, prayer and now all that has changed. You must try it, it will surprise you. I sleep very well now mainly because I have put what wisdom I have obtained to use. It is one thing to say it, but quite another to do it and to put it into practice.

Getting back to the main idea here. I honestly hope you take my plan for the year 2012 into consideration. Please remember it is your soul and the souls of your family, relatives and friends you need to be concerned with. Our goal as Roman Catholics, Christians are to get everyone to heaven. Ask your priest, he will tell you.

In fact if you feel so inclined you could dust off that old Bible and turn to the Old Testament and see for yourself what is exactly expected from you, in your short stay here on the earth. If everyone followed the Lord's direction, we would all be much better off. Check out this small excerpt I have educed for you.

Leviticus 19:18

Take no revenge and cherish no grudge against your fellow countrymen. You shall love your neighbor as yourself. I am the LORD.

- - - - - - - - - - - - - -

The Year 2012 - Here We Go Again!

How do you love your neighbor as yourself? Well, what is the best thing you could ask for yourself? How about to go to Heaven right? Sure! So, how about asking the same for everyone, your brothers and sisters. No one needs or should harbor any hate for anyone. Let us all make the journey together .....

Chapter 6

Ten Things to Remember.

I have to do this. I must emphasize this point! I wouldn't feel right unless I did. I will reiterate the fact, which I feel in my heart, is one of the biggest problems facing Roman Catholics today. We are all getting off the beaten path. We are losing the sight of the basics and we need to get on the right path again, the path of light and righteousness.

I know I don't have to say this, but I will, because I feel the need to say the things, which should get said, but never do or, at least, rarely do. I know you have heard it all before, but I think we need a refresher course in the basics. Now don't go away! I really want you to see this and review with me. Have an open mind and bear with me for a while. Please be tolerant and endure. Don't just glaze over this part, because I truly feel this is where all our problems begin.

I want you to see this addendum of the basic tenets of the Roman Catholic Church added to the end of the New American Bible, which is a compendium of the Ten Commandments.

<u>The Ten Commandments</u>

- *1. I am the LORD your God: you shall not have strange gods before me.*
- *2. You shall not take the name of the LORD your God in vain.*
- *3. Remember to keep the LORD'S day.*
- *4. Honor your father and your mother.*
- *5. You shall not kill.*
- *6. You shall not commit adultery.*
- *7. You shall not steal.*
- *8. You shall not bear false witness against your neighbor.*
- *9. You shall not covet your neighbor's wife.*
- *10. You shall not covet your neighbor's goods.*

Keep in mind the commandments listed here is not directly from scripture, but an abridged account of them and should suffice to refresh your memory. I wanted to list them here, because I was afraid to ask you to actually find, dust off and open your Holy Bibles for fear you might just skip that part.

I fear these days many people, even Roman Catholics, either don't own, never owned, can't find or have so much dust on their Holy Bibles they no longer can lift the cover to look inside. My last statement doesn't apply to everyone, of course. I know for a fact there still exists

Ten Things to Remember.

some very good Roman Catholics and Christians that wouldn't think of parting with their Holy Bibles and read them regularly. But to those of you to whom it does apply and you know who you are, we need a refresher course.

I feel sure the Ten Commandments, will bring back memories to many of you. Yes, the good old "basics", right in front of you. I know what you are thinking. You think I will proceed to go down the list explaining commandment after commandment. Wrong! My intent is not to explain the commandments, but just to have you read over them right now. Go ahead! Even if you just read them on the previous page, read them again. I want them fresh in your mind. It is very important for what I will show you next.

What really scares me are the attitudes of people, Christians and Roman Catholics alike. Many people in the categories I have just mentioned, seem to be hesitant, wavering, sometimes vacillating or even ambivalent to the commandments these days. This is not a good thing and it means we all could use some reinforcement. You can't get wishy washy when it comes to the Ten Commandments! These are black and white, there are no gray areas! If you have any doubts, you need to get yourself a "new" copy of the catechism of the Roman Catholic Church.

The "new" catechism for the Church is excellent! It leaves nothing to the imagination! This means you should have, at minimum, two books close to your side at all times, the Holy Bible and the catechism for the Roman Catholic Church. I tell you, there are some very intelligent writers in the Roman Catholic Church. They have a knack for making everything easy to read and understand. I recommend to you to have these two books. Read them, try your best to understand them and you won't go wrong. The only thing left for me to convince you of would be to add some prayer and you will be set.

I keep going off on a tangent here, but these are things which need to be said and acted on. These are some of the most important things in our lives and I believe there are a lot of us who don't even realize it. We can't keep going in this direction. We keep going farther and farther off the path of light and righteousness. If we allow ourselves to get too far off the right path, we won't be able to find it anymore!

As for me, I need to get going on the right path myself and explain why I had you read the Ten Commandments. I know you know them, at least I hope so. What I want to show you next is their importance as seen through the Lord's eyes! Just how important are the Ten Commandments? I know you personally have your ideas on their importance and that is good. Now we will see if you think the same way the Lord does about it!

You see I have figured out the Holy Bible is a wonderful instrument for understanding how the Lord "thinks". It just doesn't tell you what he has done and why he has done this or that or even what he will do. It helps you to understand how the Lord thinks and I can't over emphasize the importance of knowing this. If you have an idea on how the Lord thinks it will help you understand many other things and their importance. Now this is where what I will show you will become very important.

I think there should be attached to every exhibit of the Ten Commandments this passage from the Holy Bible:

Ten Things to Remember.

— — — — — — — — — —

Ezekiel 33:11-20

Answer them: As I live, says the Lord God, I swear I take no pleasure in the death of the wicked man, but rather in the wicked man's conversion, that he may live. Turn, turn from your evil ways! Why should you die, O house of Israel?
As for you, son of man, tell your countrymen: The virtue which a man has practiced will not save him on the day that he sins; neither will the wickedness that a man has done bring about his downfall on the day that he turns from wickedness [nor can the virtuous man, when he sins, remain alive]. Though I say to the virtuous man that he shall surely live, if he then presumes on his virtue and does wrong, none of his virtuous deeds shall be remembered; because of the wrong he has done, he shall die. And though I say to the wicked man that he shall surely die, if he turns away from his sin and does what is right and just, giving back pledges, returning stolen goods, living by the statutes that bring life, and doing no wrong, he shall surely live, he shall not die. None of the sins he committed shall be held against him; he has done what is right and just, he shall surely live. Yet your countrymen say, "The way of the Lord is not fair!"; but it is their way that is not fair. When a virtuous man turns away from what is right and does wrong, he shall die for it. But when a wicked man turns away from wickedness and does what is right and just, because of this he shall live. And still you say, "The way of the Lord is not fair!"? I will judge every one of you according to his ways, O house of Israel.

- - - - - - - - - - - - - -

Ten Things to Remember.
———————————

    I want you to read that passage real carefully. I want you to read it every time you read over the Ten Commandments. I want you to read it again, right now!

    This should give you a very good idea on how the Lord thinks! Is that how you interpret the Ten Commandments? If not, who do you think is right? You or the Lord? I bet you get that question right!

Chapter 6A

Let Us, Discuss This.

The Lord says a lot in that passage from the book of Ezekiel in the previous section. It gives you great insight on how the Lord thinks. It would do you good to read it several times! The passage is pretty straightforward, but I would like to discuss it anyway mainly to emphasize some very interesting points. It doesn't leave much to the imagination.

This lets you know exactly how the Lord is thinking and the great importance he places on the Ten Commandments. It's just I, but I think since the Lord places such great importance in the Ten Commandments, maybe, just maybe you should too! Not only that, but there are some more interesting things you may want to make note of. I truly believe this is what will separate the men from the boys. The Lord does not leave too much room for error.

The first time I read this passage it set me back a bit.

- - - - - - - - - - - - - - -

Let Us, Discuss This.

I will be honest. I knew the Ten Commandments, but I didn't quite think of them in the same way the Lord expressed them. I have since made the necessary adjustments. You may want to do the same eventually.

First of all in verse 11, the Lord tells us how, He doesn't take pleasure in sending sinners down below. He is telling us that, He loves us all and wants us all to go to Heaven. Rather, He is looking for us, the sinners to convert and to cease sinning. This is what gives the Lord pleasure! The more you read and learn about the Lord, the more you see how, He really loves us all and wants the best for us. He wants us merely to obey his commandments and be civilized to one another and be righteous and devout towards, Him, our Creator.

Is that too much to ask? To act like civilized human beings toward one another. To worship and praise, Him who gave us life. When you think about it, that is all the Ten Commandments do. They lift us out of barbarism, so we don't act like savages towards each other. You can't tell me this wouldn't be a much more wonderful world if everyone followed the Ten Commandments.

Going on to verse 12 should set you back in your chairs a bit. The Lord tells us just "one" mortal sin can erase a whole life of virtue! Once you have sinned "none" of your virtuous life is remembered! Bang! This is a grave and a verse of enormous consequences! Do you get the idea on how much emphasis our Lord places on His commandments? One mortal sin is all it takes! Did you miss Mass last week? Not a good thing!

It also works the other way. If you were a sinner all your life and from today on you convert and stop sinning you're on your way to heaven! So, if you are a sinner and if you have been one for a good long while, all is not lost. Stop sinning today and from here on, ask for forgiveness and be truly repentant of your previous sins and you go home with a clean soul.

What you should notice here, what should really stand out is "sin"! This is what is important. Just one makes all the difference! Now, how do we obtain a sin? That is correct, we break a commandment. Just one, any,

"One" commandment, is all it takes! "All" commandments are important! I don't care how good, righteous, devout or virtuous you were before or even for how long, just "one" sin could make a wash of everything!

This is why I personally believe when the Ten Commandments are taught they should be taught alongside Ezekiel 33, 11-20. You will learn to appreciate those Ten Commandments, each and every "one" of them, that much more! You should now be able to see how just one commandment, any one of them, is important to our Lord. In other words, He is not playing around, you had better pay attention, listen and get very serious!

What I see in society today is the tendency to have a very lackadaisical and apathetic attitude towards sin. Its kind of a ho-hum attitude, you know, what's the big deal anyway? Wake up and smell the coffee! Every day I see a plethora of sins passing by me from everyone, everyone! Am I the only one who sees this? I want you to spend one hour, no more, just one hour at the place where you work and count the sins that fly by. It should astound you! We are pathetic souls on this earth and we need to get back on the path of righteousness. Just count all the people in the

Let Us, Discuss This.

— — — — — — — — — — — — —

United States alone who have abortions, thousands and thousands, in fact over a million in one year! Like I said, we are pathetic!

There is only one redeeming fact, which can save us all. You need to convert now! Today! Did you know aiding and abetting a sinner is just as bad as committing the sin itself? It is! Now is the time I would like to take a moment for a little commercial. Commercial: When you knowingly aid and support a candidate for political office, whose platform includes the grievous sin of pro-choice, abortion or legalized murder, whatever you would prefer to call it, do you think you are sinning? The commercial is over. Please give that commercial a lot of thought, because I want to meet you in Heaven .....

My intention here is to place the Ten Commandments in your face and make you look at them as you may have never looked at them before! If you do that, you will thank me later in Heaven. If I have placed the fear of God in you, I have succeeded. If not, there is more work I need to do. You can't just blow off the Ten Commandments! They are serious! They separate the men from the boys! Just an expression, no offense to the ladies out there.

Just a simple thing as using the Lords name in vain can really heat up your eternal life to the max! I use that as an example, because I hear it all the time, my suggestion is if and when you feel the urge to commit a disgusting sin such as this try and learn to replace it with a good, "praise the Lord" phrase instead. It fits in much better and leaves you with a much cleaner soul.

Finally, still working my way through the previous passage, the Lord makes another statement, which bears

- - - - - - - - - - - - - -

sitting up and taking notice to. He states he will judge "everyone" of us according to our ways. The important things are the word "everyone". There are no exceptions! I get the impression many people think if they do a good deed here and a good deed there, that in itself will excuse them of their other sins. Wrong! Good deeds don't take-away sins, rather, sins take-away the good deeds! It's real important you appreciate the difference!

Obeying the Ten Commandments is our duty. The duty assigned to us by the Lord. Generally speaking it isn't too hard to do our duty when everything is going good, but tends to get very difficult when they are not. However, in either case, good or bad, they must be followed and you now know, if you didn't before, the importance the Lord places on following them. Yet, we are not done.

Our great Lord also expects us to let everyone know this and their importance. We are to act as his disciples and clue everyone in, get them informed. Our goal should not only be to follow the Ten Commandments, but to get everyone around us to do so. You need to show your love for your brothers and sisters and not only do what is necessary to get you to heaven, but everyone around you, everyone. This is what will make you worthy of calling you yourself a Roman Catholic, a Christian. If you do that and if I ask you, "You have the nerve to call yourself a Roman Catholic!" You can reply, "I most certainly do!"

This is where the title of this book is derived. I was watching a very well known politician, proclaiming the greatness of "pro-choice" and in almost in the same mouthful professing the fact that she was a Roman Catholic. This is where I said, "You have the nerve to call yourself a Roman Catholic!". I couldn't believe my ears! You can't be serious, can you? The worst of it was, she was serious! Disgusting! Lady, don't say something like that and then try at the same time to say you are a Roman Catholic, please! I couldn't believe my ears. What kind of sense is this?

I know most of you have seen and heard all of what I have said before. You can't escape it, it's everywhere and getting worse! You need to draw a line somewhere and do something about it. Even if you are not guilty of any of the above and lead a most virtuous life you are not on an island shielded from everyone else. I would think if you are that virtuous person you would want to be surrounded by the same. How do we do that? Is it even possible?

We definitely can do that and anything is possible, when you have the Lord on your side! We, us Christians, us Roman Catholics need to work together and take action against the evil in this country and in this world. I have no doubt in my mind that the good Lord will back us if he sees us trying to fight the evil in this world. If he sees us doing nothing, but sitting on our duffs, I'm not sure what our Lord would do. I'm pretty sure the last scenario wouldn't thrill Him. Picture yourself on judgement day and the Lord asks you what you have you done about all the evil, which was around you. You can't lie in the face of the Lord, He knows all and sees all. When you tell Him you didn't do diddly squat, you think it will put a smile on His face?

Speaking of judgement day, maybe this is something we should be discussing. What will you say on that momentous and grand day? "Well, I didn't think "all" the

Let Us, Discuss This.

— — — — — — — — — —

commandments were that important, but I didn't kill anyone." Yes, that sounds pretty good. Yeah, right!

The way I like to think is always in respect to judgement day. This is "my" thinking personally, but you may want to take heed anyway. I always have in the back of my mind that day, judgement day. It's a day which is coming for everyone. I always think when I do anything of how it will look for the Lord on that day. I want the Lord to have the look of approval when he goes through the list of deeds on my life's journey, not a scowl. Every time you even think about breaking a commandment you should reflect on judgement day. This is the most important time of your life! Above everything else! Forget about the year 2012 and think about something that is really important!

Judgement day is what will take you into eternity. You only get one chance to screw it up. One mortal sin is all it takes. You better read that passage from Ezekiel a few more times. I say things like this to people and they think it is a joke. It's all fun and games until judgement day gets here and it can be at any time for any one of us.

I want you to remember an old guy with gray hair told you this. Don't make me say, "I told you so!" When the time comes I would rather have you say, "Boy, I'm sure glad I listened to that old guy with the gray hair!"

I want to ask you a favor. Every time you or any one in your family should think of the Ten Commandments or any commandment at all, for any reason whatsoever, I want you to read the passage I showed you from the Book of *Ezekiel 33:11-20.* At least think of that passage in your mind. If that doesn't straighten you out, I will pray for you, because you will need my prayer! Why do I say this?

- - - - - - - - - - - - - -

Let Us, Discuss This.

I say this because I want to say the things which need to be said and never seem to get said, but should. I care and you should too. The Lord doesn't think of the commandments as a joking matter, in fact he couldn't be more serious. After reading this I hope all of you do the same. It will be the healthiest decision you ever made in your life for your soul. The soul is what counts .....

Chapter 7

The House of the Lord.

B y now you should be getting to know me rather well. Rightly so, because I'm spilling my guts out to you, revealing to you my real "inner" self, how I feel inside, how I think, everything. Believe it or not, I normally don't complain at all or rarely anyway. I don't like being a complainer. I like more to be one who compliments. If you can, I believe it is the best way to be. Nonetheless, there comes a time when you feel you have to say something, especially if it is done in a way to improve a person or that persons' environment.

This is that time. The house of the Lord, our Church. We should be very thankful for the Church. This is where we receive the body and blood of our Lord Jesus Christ. The best structure built by human hands you could ever possibly have the privilege to enter. People should be busting the doors down to get inside, but alas, they are not. As I observe, they are doing quite the opposite. They appear to be busting the doors down, because they can't

- - - - - - - - - - - - - -

seem to wait to get out. Shame, shame on you, Roman Catholics! I fear we are losing the reverence we should have when we attend Church and I believe we should look to correct the problem.

Again, this is my personal opinion and you may accept it for what it is worth. I get the feeling we are missing some sincerity when we fulfill the duties of our religion. Maybe I'm the only one who feels this way, but I feel sincerity is a huge factor when it comes to religion. I think of the confessional a lot, because it helps me to gauge how genuine and honest I might be acting.

Normally when you go to confession, confess your sins and leave, you should feel better about yourself. After all your sins have been forgiven. Your soul is clean! I did say "normally". Lets say you weren't very "sincere" with your confession. You purposely failed to confess that you stole someone's watch, because you were embarrassed by your sin. Your confession wasn't complete, honest and genuine and your soul is not yet clean. Confession only works for the sincere, for those who give a genuine confession, a confession from the heart!

I wonder if going to Church might work in somewhat the same way? Are you attending Church because someone, say your parents, are forcing you to? Maybe you are there "only" to obey the first precept, doctrine or rule of the Church? Are you paying attention to what is going on while in Church? Do you participate in the activities during Mass? If you don't pay attention during the mass are you being sincere? If you don't participate during the mass are you being sincere? If you are only going to Mass because it is required by the first precept of the Church are you being sincere? If your not sincere at Mass does Mass help you at all?

Catechism of the Catholic Church

P.493, Paragraph 2042:

The first precept ("You shall attend Mass on Sundays and on holy days of obligation and rest from servile labor").

There is nothing wrong with obeying the five precepts of the Roman Catholic Church. I wonder how many know all "five" precepts of the Church? Anyway, the point is, with the Church's first precept, not only attendance, but "reverence" should be the order of the day. In other words, you should not simply attend in body, but also in "soul". Just being there is not enough! What you should have, is a deep feeling of profound awe, respect and even love pouring out from you when crossing the threshold of the doors. You should be participating in the Mass and concentrating on every word of the celebrant, priest or bishop, who is presiding at the Mass. You should bring your heart and soul to Mass.

I think a few things are possible when observing the members of our Churches. Either people don't remember, they are uninformed and don't know, or they don't believe that one "extremely important" person is in attendance at every Mass. It has to be true. It is the only way in my mind I can justify the actions of many of the parishioners of the Church. It saddens me to even think about it. I speak not about one or two people here, but many, too many!

The person I speak of is the Lord Jesus Himself, he is in attendance at every mass. If you believe and you better, He is there at every Mass. Knowing this to be true is where I have problems observing others at mass and trying to explain their actions. I say this, because if you do believe, I believe you would never act the way you do! He is there! At every Mass!

I can't believe the people at mass do what they do and know or believe the Lord Jesus is among them! If they do, they have a bizarre way of showing it.

Matthew 18:20

"For where two or three are gathered together in my name, there am I in the midst of them."

Those are not my words. Those are the words of Jesus. Now, either we believe in him or we don't. Right now I want to go on record as one who believes! If you believe and know this, explain to me your actions. I hope you are not doing one of those, "Yeah, yeah, yeah I believe" things. If you are, you're in a lot of trouble and better start examining your ways! This is where everything comes to a head. You can't tell me you believe and act the way you do. I will tell you what I see and I think you will understand why I feel the way I do.

I must say one important thing. Not everyone I see at Mass falls into this category, but there are many, many who do. I don't know if it was always this way, but I hope and pray it wasn't. I will go through the list of infractions, so to speak and then you can tell me what you think. The only other possible reason I could come up with is that you just don't care or you really are just a body taking up space in the pew and are in your own world when it comes to your mind, body and soul. Those explanations won't do you much good either.

It is like everyone is simply going through the motions, even if they do that much, then going home never to think of the Church again until another 167 hours pass, only to repeat the same once again. I don't know what you want to call it, but I don't call that much of a religious way to perform.

I think what should happen is that the Roman Catholic Church needs to start a class on how to properly enter a Church and to attend mass. I believe many of us would need a refresher course and even some more education in our religion before they could pass the test for that class. I imagine often the problem could be plain old ignorance, no disrespect intended, you don't know if no one tells you or a lack of any incentive to learn.

I speak of very simple things, but necessary things. I see many people who don't know or care how to properly enter the Church itself. Should be a simple thing right? Well, maybe not that simple. First of all you should be on time. I know that might not be always possible and it is better to be late then not to come at all. Personally I put in my mind the Mass starts fifteen minutes before it actually does. If I would normally have been five minutes late, I end up ten minutes early instead. I should mention coming early is a good thing. It is good, because it will give you a chance to say some prayers before the mass starts, but

— — — — — — — — — — —

what is even better is it gives you a chance to actually converse with God. Remember he is there, so speak to him. Tell Him how the past week went. Tell Him what you would like and need. Thank him for all he has done for you. Talking with God is prayer you know. Also keep in mind, when you pray you are talking to "someone", not "something", there is a difference.

I have to stop right now and tell you I know for a fact prayer does work. It may even be the subject for my next book. Ask and you shall receive. If you don't ask, guess what? If you are late, you are late, but do your best to get to mass on time. It's really a big distraction when someone comes in late, especially if they are clumsy and banging all around. If you have to be late do your best to enter quietly.

Oh, before I forget. How about coming in the proper attire. This is one of the most abused things I see in Church. I'm not saying you need to come to Church in a coat and tie or even in an evening gown for the women, but come on people I know we could do better than what I have seen! You want to go to see the Lord looking like that? I know you can't see the lord when you are in Church but, He is there. It is a lot like air, you know it is there, in fact everywhere, but you can't see it can you? Same idea. Imagine if he did appear in the flesh, right there in Church, right in front of you, you know, he's done it before. Do you want Him to see you like you were dressed last week? Wouldn't you want to look your best? I know I speak to about half of the congregation, when I say this. You should be dressing your best to show the Lord some respect. Would you go to a job interview looking the way you do in Mass? I think probably not. If that would be true, it would mean you would dress up for your interview, but not for your Creator? Maybe we need to review our priorities?

You may ask, "What do you mean by dressing with respect?" I will tell you what it doesn't mean, it doesn't mean a teenage girl wearing slacks with a slogan I won't repeat embroidered across her rump! I seen that just this week. It doesn't mean wearing jeans with holes in the knees and elsewhere! It doesn't mean blouses showing the midriff! It doesn't mean tennis shoes or sneakers! I can go on and on and on.

What it "does" mean is wearing a clean pair of dress slacks and a dress shirt for the guys and no hats on while inside the Church. The shirt and pants do not have to be anything fancy, just clean and neat. The women a nice "conservative" dress, proper length or clean slacks and a decent blouse would be fine. Again, nothing fancy, just clean and neat. I don't want to sound like a prude or anything, but you are going to be in the presence of the Lord. I would think that alone commands at least a little respect. Finally some dress shoes for all the males and females and you would have a congregation everyone could be proud of.

Let me add one thing to the dress code. I firmly believe anyone who wants and needs to enter Church should be allowed to enter regardless of their attire. I say this as long as it is within reason of course, for instance, naked, no or caked all over in mud, no. If your truly down to your last dollar and only have the clothes on your back, ok.

I seriously doubt, the people I speak of, are so extremely poor they can't afford a set or so of dress clothes from one of the department store chains for Sunday, but if you can't, then fine, forget I said anything. I try not to be hard to get along with. All of what I have said is just in the name of common decency and respect for our Lord.

Ok we managed to get in the door, with our nice clean dress clothes, next you should bless yourself with holy water. I don't see many violators of this little, but powerful ritual. It seems to be one thing that has caught on even in these troubled times. Once in a while there may be a violator, but most of us do at least that much. For those of you who don't know "why" you bless yourself with holy water, like I was for many years, I will tell you. I was just told you're supposed to do it and that's it and shut up. Many of us assume everyone knows the simplest of customs and rules in the Church and during the Mass, but many of us would be "wrong" at the same time.

When you bless yourself with the holy water and make the sign of the cross you are manually recalling your baptism. The font you dip your fingers into has water in it, which has been blessed itself and is "holy" and is what you are using to bless "yourself" with. A little bit of religious trivia there. Manually recalling your baptism means you are reaffirming your faith and again claim that you are Christ's by making His sign, over your body, with the waters of baptism. The water was blessed at Easter Vigil and used for baptizing the catechumens and now by you, who is reaffirming your faith. You should reaffirm your faith every time you enter Church, especially for mass. It should be done with grand and meaningful reverence, thoughtfulness and gratitude.

The House of the Lord.

— — — — — — — — — —

There are many of these little rituals and customs we perform when entering the Church and at Mass, which are very spiritually rich and shine in the reverence of the Lord. I fear many of those little things tend to get skipped or not emphasized properly as to their importance. So, I can't blame everything on the people. They may have never been taught these things themselves or were taught by someone "behind the barn somewhere" and never received "proper" instructions. Another thing I find missing is many times when we teach our children to do these things we don't always explain the "why" factor and they never realize their importance. Always teach the "why" factor, it helps the child, or any person for that matter, to really appreciate the significance of these customs. Always remember there is a reason for everything, if you don't know that reason you should attempt to seek it out.

We have entered the Church on time, in our nice clean dress clothes and blessed ourselves. Good start so far. Next, we need to learn how to take our seat. You need to find a pew which has room or is empty. Once a place has been found, you should genuflect towards the tabernacle (one knee all the way to the floor), which contains the Blessed Sacrament, the real presence of Jesus Christ, to which you are paying homage in giving only the best of your honor and respect to Him. As you do this, you should also be making a very reverent sign of the cross. This would be considered to be an act of "adoration". A "good" thing! We are assuming the sanctuary lamp is lit, if not, a profound bow (bending forward at the waist) will suffice and would be considered an act of "reverence". Also, a "good" thing.

- - - - - - - - - - - - - -

The House of the Lord.

— — — — — — — — — — — —

Finally you would step into the pew, put the kneeler down, make the sign of the cross again and kneel. Here is where you may begin prayer and conversing with God until Mass begins assuming you entered Church early enough to take advantage of some additional prayer. Another "good" thing whenever possible.

This is "my" take on the proper way to conduct yourselves, enter the Church and to prepare for the start of the Mass. Do you think I'm being unreasonable? I sincerely hope not. It may be a little extra work, but remember you are doing this to show your deepest respect for our Lord. I don't think that is asking too much.

I won't go through the entire Mass, except saying, you should also be responding properly to all the prayers and participating in the singing of the hymns or songs appropriately throughout the mass. This is not a good time to be napping! I get between four and five, usually closer to four, hours of sleep before Mass, due to my work. I believe others may own a similar situation. It could and generally is not very easy to remain alert under those circumstances. I bring my little mini Bible and follow along with the readings to help. Yes, that means you must do a little extra work and book mark the lectionary reading's for the day before you get to Mass in order to find the reading quick enough.

Once the Mass has ended, it wouldn't hurt to linger for a while and say a few more prayers, maybe for your advantage or your families. It would really be good to break out and dust off that Rosary and meditate on one of the mysteries of our faith. I Know this isn't always possible, because at many Churches, when one Mass

- - - - - - - - - - - - -

— — — — — — — — — —

comes to an end, a later Mass may be getting ready to start.

In any event, we should not be breaking down the doors of the Church to get out, when the Mass has ended! Generally the pastor waits at the front door after Mass, which presents a very good opportunity for you to introduce yourself to him and maybe tender the possibility of conducting a little tet-a-tet before leaving.

The best thing you do all week is to attend Mass at your Church. We need to get back to the basics and understand the great gift the Lord has given us. If we do it right, we leave Mass with a clean soul and much closer to God every week. We need to remember our lives on Earth are real short, even if we would live to be one hundred and fifty years old, it is nothing compared to an eternity with God, hopefully! We only get one chance on Earth to do things right and now would not be a good time to blow it! We need to teach our children the same and I mean "really" teach them. Take the time to not only teach and instruct, but to learn those "why" factors and learn a deep respect and admiration for our Lord and the Roman Catholic Mass. If your children tell you they are bored at Mass you haven't done a good enough job in explaining it to them. Make them not only attend Mass, but see, feel and appreciate what is inside those doors, so much so, they will want to share their experience with their friends.

What I have explained to you in the few words of this section are some of the basics. Why did I do that? Shouldn't almost everyone know the basics? I will tell you why I have done this and I think most of you will agree with me. It's the evidence. There is none! Ok, I will retract

- - - - - - - - - - - - - -

— — — — — — — — — — —

"none", but very little. If you go to Church, it's hard to find people observing the basics to give you the "evidence" or proof of the basics being known.

What is so great about knowing the basics? I feel the more you know of the basics of our religion the more everything else will fall in place for you. The more you will be able to cope with and understand things later, when things aren't so easy to digest or comprehend. When you have a good understanding of the basics, it will help you appreciate the rich heritage of our Church from the beginning with our first Pope until now, engraved with glorious splendor in traditions, rites and customs to be renowned. The understanding of even the simplest of things in the Church and in the Mass can grow inside you a fruitful tree of appreciation you will cherish and hold in the greatest esteem for the remainder of your lives. If you don't have the basics, it will be very hard, maybe even impossible, for that to happen. If you don't have the basics, you don't have anything to build on and to grow with.

Going beyond the basics should be the goal of everyone. If you are like me, the more you learn, the more you want to learn and the more you will appreciate how lucky we are to be a part of this grand institution. The Holy Bible is obviously a book you can spend your entire life studying and building your knowledge with, but there are other very helpful books you can use to get through the basics and much more than the basics. First on the list of everyone should be the basics, but it's just the "first" thing on the list, there will always be more. You will never run out of material to learn from, to enjoy and marvel at.

- - - - - - - - - - - - - -

The House of the Lord.

‒ ‒ ‒ ‒ ‒ ‒ ‒ ‒ ‒ ‒ ‒

I would like to suggest one point of caution for you. When reading other books make sure they have the approval of the Church, so you get it right the first time. You need to be aware and make sure you are absorbing the correct and most congruent information. The best way to do that is to make sure it is written or at least approved by the Roman Catholic Church.

Grow in your knowledge of the basics and then use the basics to amplify and enrich your life with knowledge and the wisdom of our Lord and you will be one happy Roman Catholic! I have found it makes you a more confident and happy person, but most of all it helps you to cope with the day no matter what it brings, because you will realize the Lord is right beside you and there is nothing you and Him can't handle! You learn to really start appreciating "all" the gifts the Lord has given you and there are many, regardless of your particular situation. Want to have a smile that will last for the rest of your life? Sure you do. Commit the following line to memory:

True happiness is being satisfied and very thankful for all the Lord has given you.

Write that last line down and don't forget it! Teach it to your children, make them truly understand it! This is some of that "wisdom" stuff! You're welcome. This is your big payoff on Earth and there is much, much more after that and beyond .....

Chapter 8

What is a Christian Anyway?

Amazing, totally amazing! Are we teaching our children anything? Are we even talking to our children? I wouldn't have believed it if I hadn't witnessed it myself, but it's true. Shame on you, Roman Catholics, shame on you! Shame on you, other Christians, shame on you too! None of you are doing your duty! At least, not by my tabulations so far.

In the performance of my job I come in contact with and work with teenagers many a time. If you remember, earlier I stated I like to bring up religion in the workplace. I won't go back on that statement. Normally the way I go about it, at least with regards to my first contact with a person, I will ask them if they are a Christian. Just out of the clear blue. It is not a question that should offend anyone and if they are new to the job it is the kind of thing which breaks the ice of newness and leads to some interesting discussions at times. I will tell you this,

- - - - - - - - - - - - - -

sometimes in life you don't always get what you think you will get or what you planned for. This would be one of those times.

This should not be a difficult question. I repeat, This should not be a difficult question. Yeah right! This is where I get amazed. When I ask this of a teenager, which most often I will. I see this glazed look or stare in their eyes, since this happens approximately 99.9% of the time, I instantly know what it means without a word being said. This wasn't true at first, but experience has furnished me with the answer before the answer is ever stated or better said, confessed. The glazed look means they have no clue! They don't even understand the question most of the time! Following the glazed look comes the most familiar answer, "no".

Now, judging by the look, the glazed eyes and already knowing they have no idea what I have just asked them my next question invariably will be, "Then, you don't believe in Jesus?" Which, inevitably yields the response, "Oh, I believe in Jesus!" Now, if you didn't know any better, which is the way I was when I first starting asking these questions, my next response would have been and probably yours, "What?" However, being a veteran of this particular line of questioning and knowing the subject, the teenager, has no clue whatsoever, I now proceed to say, "You do know that a Christian is one who believes in Jesus right?" I usually say that, that way, as not to embarrass them too much and their typical response is, "I guess so." All right then, we have a "winner"!

This doesn't happen once or twice, but "always"! If you don't believe me, try it yourself. Talk about the

What is a Christian Anyway?

"mysteries" of faith! I speak of children from the ages of say, fourteen to twenty. What I really hate to say is I could put a good number of adults in the same category! This is not a good thing. Something even more amazing is that a few, not many, but a few teenagers become a bit frightened at just the question itself! I instantly get the impression they have the notion it is really a bad thing to be talking religion in the work place.

Heaven forbid, I should ask them what religion they follow! Guess what? Most of them can't even answer that question! If they do answer, they can't tell me a thing about their religion or what they believe. This is totally and completely disgusting! What now? Do we keep our teenagers in the closet, only to let them out to eat? What do you do when you get these type responses? Of course, you already knowing I profess to be a veteran in the course of this type of questioning, you should already suspect I have a good answer to the last question I solicited. Since I'm a veteran and earned my stripes already, the answer would be yes, but not till after much anguish has passed.

What I do next is to "educate" them. Being an ex college professor, it comes out naturally in me. My problem is I should "not" have to do this! This is horrible! This tells me these children are being raised without any religion! If you can't tell me if you are a Christian or not or even what religion you practice, you are without religion. This brings me to a great sorrow for these children, because they have no idea what they are missing!

Understand, I don't force any religion on them, but I do explain to them what my previous questions meant and define the word "Christian" to them. At least then they will understand that much. If they ask more of me I will continue to educate them, but only if they should ask. I don't want to get their parents upset, should it be a problem and I would never force anything on them. The most I might try to do is to explain the Roman Catholic religion to them if they would ask and tell them, since I'm a Roman Catholic, it would be the religion I would know best. Only to inform them, not to convert them. This is my rule for children, but not necessarily for adults.

What is America going to be like in twenty more years? Will anyone know of religion? Will religion be extinct? When I was a kid growing up everyone, knew their religion and most everyone practiced their religion. Do you think we are heading in the right direction? When I first started asking these types of questions, I never even imagined I would get the responses I was getting. I never imagined getting the same response from everyone!

Tell me why everyone is afraid to speak about their religion in public, outside of their family! We do still have freedom of speech, correct? I guess it has always been in the back of my mind, until now that is, that "almost" everyone in the United States believed in God and the Ten Commandments bare minimum. There are some exceptions to every rule. They may not have obeyed the Ten Commandments, but at least they acknowledged them and their existence. What that did for me was to give me a kind of warm feeling inside, knowing I belonged to a God-fearing country and was surrounded by others who felt the same basic way. Now I'm not sure. I never really sat down and thought about it at that time, but looking back to those times I realize the feeling was there, inside, in the background, in my heart, always. I never realized what I was missing, till it was taken away.

The feeling isn't there anymore, it's gone and it scares me. I believe it scares me, because I know with the feeling gone, there is something missing, which is something really good and the feeling should be there. I want that feeling back! I'm as serious as anyone could be. I never knew it before this, but I banked on that feeling, counted on it being there. I feel the same in my heart as always, but this feeling I speak of was an extra perk, so to speak and made me feel just that much better inside. It's gone. I need you to help me get it back. It will make you feel better inside too. If you never felt what I speak of, you need to, it's a good feeling and everyone should feel it. The feeling adds warmth to your soul and that cold, cruel world, isn't so cold anymore, because you know inside it isn't as cruel.

These people, these children need to find God inside, to feel and appreciate Him. We will all do better, because of it. The United States wasn't perfect when I was a child, but the "feeling" was there and I believe many had the feeling, even if they didn't sit back and acknowledge it, it was there. When it is taken away it leaves a hole in your heart, your soul and if you are like me, you need to mend that hole to get that wonderful feeling back.

Those were the days when you could leave your front door unlocked at night and go to sleep without worry. When you could send your children off to school in the morning a half a mile away and not give it an extra thought. If you are older, you know what I speak of, if not, it's a shame, a real shame. You knew your neighbors, you knew everyone in the neighborhood and you trusted them and they looked out for you and you looked out for them.

You had block parties. The police would come and actually block off traffic to your block for the whole day in the summer. Everyone in the block would break out their grills and put them right in the middle of the street and be cooking hot dogs and burgers or maybe chicken. The night before the women would make pies, cakes and other type desserts and bring them out to the party. Everyone shared the food, deserts and the drink. There were music, dancing and singing. The entire block participated for the whole day. If you didn't know the family at the other end of the block, you got to know them then. All the children played together, everyone was in harmony with everyone else!

You got to try Mary's famous apple pie, at least famous in our block. You watched as Henry showed you his trained pigeons and how he could release them and let them fly away, only to return again in about fifteen minutes, all of them! You had to have some of Barbera's grilled sausage, she was Billy's and Linda's mother who lived in the bright yellow house. Some of the guys would break out the checker board, some others the horse shoes. The ladies would be showing each other the sewn creations they made for their children and exchanging recipes. Food and drink, soda, ice tea and for sure beer (only for the adults). Everyone had a great time! They're bellies full and their friends and neighbors all in glorious splendor enjoying the beautiful day. Everyone enjoyed each others company. When you heard there was going to be a "block party" coming soon it would make your day.

When we speak of the good old days, this is what us

older fogies are talking about. If you participated in block parties back then, you are sure to be missing them today. Then, is when you had that "feeling" inside and it was at its apex, its highest point, its maximum peak. They were all God-fearing people and you knew it, they didn't have to say it. This is the feeling, this is what is missing. It gave you an extra sense of security. It helped you to act more neighborly and everyone lived a more enriched life. God was with us.

You take God away you end up with what we have now. Locked front doors. You must escort your children every inch of the way to school. You don't know your next door neighbor's name, much less the neighbor at the other end of the block. No more block parties, no more sharing of food and drink and being social with one and another. We lived back then, we exist now. Oh and everyone was just as broke as everyone else, but we all shared. Everyone shared. You could go half way down the block and you could ask Ed to spot you a twenty till payday and he would. Ed knew he would get the money back and he would. If it was going to be a real problem Ed would tell you just to keep it and that would be it. Not just Ed, but most everyone was that way. If you were especially broke, everyone on the block helped you out with food, drink and even some cash to tide you over, until things got better. The best thing is no one took advantage of the hospitality, but they knew it was there if they needed it. It was the way it should be, you even had that "feeling" and you didn't even know it. You know, the feeling which is missing now, but shouldn't be. We had the Lord with us, now our children don't even know of

What is a Christian Anyway?

Him, His name even. What have we gotten ourselves into? Where are we going? We need to get the "feeling" back. I think there is a connection between that feeling and the Lord, maybe, just maybe, that feeling is the Lord inside us.

No, everything was not perfect back then. You had sinners then, you have sinners now. It was different, however, much different. Maybe if you had attended a block party you would understand better. If you never had the "feeling" I guess you really couldn't know. About the closest I get to that feeling today is Church picnics and other Church events. Maybe there is a connection there. Also, I get the impression today people think they have to act like animals to have a good time. If they are not breaking the law or a commandment or two, they are not having fun. I truly feel sorry for them. They are pushing the Lord away instead of trying to get that feeling inside, that great feeling.

My suggestion is to organize a block party this summer or two or three of them, but "first" give your children, relatives and friends the gift of religion, the wonderful Roman Catholic religion! Yes, you will have to explain to your children what a Christian is, please. Yes, you will have to go out and introduce yourself to everyone on your block and invite them to the block party and explain to, most of them anyway, exactly what a block party is. Yes, you will have to get a permit from the police department to block off your block for the day. That is one thing you need to do today, you didn't have to do back then, that is to pay for a permit. You will have to make up some rules, so as to keep the party from getting out of hand and so you won't have anyone acting like animals. You may need to educate some on how to have fun and not to act like an animal at the same time.

It would be great therapy and maybe it will help you to get that feeling inside for once or to get it back if you had it, then lost it. No matter what, in the end, you will end up with a better "feeling" inside and you will understand what I'm talking about. Try it, you'll like it.

We need to start reaching out to people. They need to know what a Christian is. It is necessary! We will all do better because of it, I'm sure. Just because a person has no religion, doesn't mean they necessarily don't want religion. If you are never told, you will never know. It just might be they need someone to enlighten them. Maybe you are the one to do that. It is your duty as a Christian and a Roman Catholic.

Why do you think a lot of people do the things they do? I will bet many of the times it is because they haven't been exposed to religion. You know, like those teenagers I question, the ones with that glazed look in their eyes. Yes, them, those are the ones alright .....

Chapter 8A

We Need a Dinner Table!

This is the key right here. We need a dinner table and we need one badly! We need to talk to our children, to have at least one meal a day where the entire family can sit down and discusses things important to them and where we could begin to get some religion into them.

The best would be to have three meals together every day, but we need at least one. This, the lack of communication, is another thing I have noticed while questioning teenagers at work. We are not communicating with our children. It is obvious! It is not good!

I know I said a meal and for some people that may be almost impossible. I know how it can be these days, working two jobs, working strange hours, working many hours, working a great distance from the home. If it is not possible, then you need to set aside a time of the day to communicate with your children, even if it is for only a

- - - - - - - - - - - - - - -

small amount of time on some days. It has to be done and it is necessary.

Many times I can't believe my ears, what I hear and what I don't hear. Sometimes I will ask teenagers what their father does for a living. Do you know how many times they don't know the answer to that question? More times than I care to say! How can you possibly be a teenager and not know what your father does for a living? Well, there are many. What does this tell me? It tells me there is no communication. It also probably tells me this teenager is one of those with the glazed eyes!

It also tells me we are not doing our duty as a Christian and we need to read our catechism books again! This is not a rare instance for me, In fact I find it quite commonplace. It's happening all around me like a sickness. We absolutely need to fix this problem before it is too late! Obviously if they can't tell me where their father is employed, it is highly probable they can't tell me anything about their religion or at least not much.

We need to unite with our children. They are the next generation. They will be raising your grandchildren! You need to teach them a lot of things and above all and at the very minimum the basics of their religion. They need to understand the Ten Commandments, not just to recite them. They need to understand the sanctity of life and how to discern and recognize evil even when that evil becomes a law! How will they ever know this unless you instruct them? Do you want them to figure it out for themselves? I hope not and good luck with that type of thinking.

One of the basics in our religion is in the family unit. We have to do the best to keep our families together and make it a haven or place of refuge for our children to know they can always come back to and learn and beget wisdom from whenever they deem it necessary. This will give them the confidence, strength and knowledge to flap their wings and to go off into the cold, cruel world and not just survive, but make it a better place.

I was very fortunate as a child. My parents made a very good team. My mother was always my back an inspiration for going forward and my father was great at leading me down the righteous path and instilling in my mind virtuous ways to be and act towards. I will always be in their debt and will always blame them for all the good that have transpired from my person. They taught me to discern right from wrong although I didn't always follow their direction and payed the price because of it. They were by no means perfect, but then which of us are? Despite their imperfections I will always feel I was blessed with the best set of parents a person could have.

If you make your children feel this way and understand those basics of our religion you will have done an excellent job. If not you have your work to do and cut out for you. It will be an objective consuming your entire life, but very satisfying when you see the results of your labors. This is your duty as a Christian of the Roman Catholic faith and a fantastic way of showing your love for your children and helping in their success in life and their spirituality.

Much of what I just said can be done at the dinner table, not all, but a preponderance. It really doesn't have to be at the dinner table, but normally there everyone in the family feels comfortable and at ease. Also, there should be no distractions, no TV on in the background, no music unless it is set low and is something soothing. You don't want any distractions or as few as possible. Now is the time for some serious communication.

You are not discussing the weather. You want to have "meaningful" discussions to find out exactly what your children know and what they don't know, but maybe should. Find out how they feel, let them know how you feel. Determine and discuss what the "why's" are and the "what ifs" could be. Make sure they are progressing in our faith and they understand and correctly interpret what has been taught. You need to give them a full understanding of the basics of our faith with emphasis on marriage, family, the Ten Commandments and the sanctity of life to mention a few.

I remember watching a western movie with my father. In one of the scenes of the movie the bad guys were beating up a priest. Well, my father was appalled and he said to me, "You see that there, don't you ever disrespect or lay a hand on a priest! In fact, I will tell you this, never disrespect a priest or nun and never, ever disrespect your mother. They are all at the top of the list! Actually you should never disrespect anyone, but especially the ones I have already mentioned. Respect everyone, even if you feel they don't deserve it. If you show respect, even to the people who don't respect you three things happen. One, you will show and teach them the proper way to act. Two, you will leave your actions in their memories and given time they might just change their ways. Three, you will be acting as a Christian, which is your duty."

All of that from a movie scene. Something I have never

We Need a Dinner Table!
— — — — — — — — — — —

forgot and never will. This was communication and it wasn't even at the dinner table! The dinner table may be where your communication with your children begins, but it should also be sought at every available opportunity. It should also be a continuing and ongoing process, never ending.

When I was about six years old, I was playing with some kids in the neighborhood and it just so happened one of them was black. Soon after we were playing one of the other children's mothers came and seen her child playing with the black kid, hauled him off and began scolding him, because he was playing with a black kid.

The lady knew my mother and seen me playing too and went to my house. I had already gone back home and seen her coming. She knocked on my door and my mother came and opened the door for her. She told my mother, "Did you know your son was playing with a black kid?" Well, my mother went off and I can't tell you everything she said, but I can give you an idea. Basically she said, "So what! My son can play with anyone he wants to. What is wrong with my son playing with a black kid anyway?" That was enough, the lady left with her tail between her legs and I learned a very valuable lesson.

Later my mother explained to me that everyone is equal and I could play with anyone I want. She also told me not to listen to the other kid's mother, because she was acting incorrectly and to let her know if anything like that ever happens again.

Do you think I learned anything here? I did and in action, right on the battlefield. That lesson was branded into my memory banks forever. Actually, at first, I thought

We Need a Dinner Table!

I was going to get in real trouble for playing with that black kid, little did I know how my mother was going to respond. These are the kind of things mothers and fathers should be doing all the time, besides normal communications at the dinner table.

Any communication is good and anywhere, anytime. The dinner table is where you may begin, but seize the opportunity whenever necessary and prudent and you will be raising some fine children. Your children need this until they're of age and have received a good helping of the basics taught by you. This is why the family unit is so important.

I have given you just a couple of examples of some of my learning experiences, but there are many more. The reason I used those particular examples is, because they were some of the ones really burned into my mind like a branding iron and ones I will never forget. You want a bunch of those for your child to be able to tap into, when the situation requires it. It works best when both parents, mother and father, are there, because they together will be able to give their child a well-rounded education of religion and life wisdom for the child to delve into and arm themselves with, when going out into the world on their own.

My problem is I don't see this happening. If I did, I wouldn't be saying anything about it. It is crucial that this step is not ignored in raising our children. How will they know these things if we don't teach them? The answer is they won't. I see it all the time and it saddens me greatly. It makes me very thankful for how I was raised. My parents took the time, even though they had five children.

We Need a Dinner Table!

Depending on the child, it may seem what you say goes in one ear and out the other. They hear, they just don't always want to obey. Getting them to obey may take more time. I know they hear, because often as my daughters were growing up I would hear them repeat to each other some of the same things I told them, but thought they would never learn. What you say to them will get in there and when they get older and more mature it begins to work its wonders. It took my daughters until they graduated high school and then it all fell in place. They have become wonderful daughters a father can really be proud of.

Every child is different, some catch on quickly and for some it may take a while, so don't get frustrated. In any case you need to keep on teaching them and emphasizing the religion in their lives. Tell them this:

The Lord is much like the air around us. The air is all around us, it is everywhere. Even though we can't see it, it is there, we know it is there, because we are breathing. The Lord is everywhere too, you can't see him, but he is there, we know He is there, because we are breathing.

I believe your children will appreciate the above. It was said in an earlier chapter, but warrants repeating. It will give them something to think about and value.

Take advantage of the fact that the Lord is with you always. Speak to him, he will get you through anything and everything. Remember your religion, the basics, the commandments. He will see you get everything you need for the moment and more.

We Need a Dinner Table!

— — — — — — — — — — —

We need to believe if we want our religion to work or have faith. Having faith is believing. You have to always keep in mind, when you walk through life the Lord is right beside you and is there to always help you. It is when we forget this that things happen or when we really don't believe. You will walk with much more confidence if you always remember that simple little fact and truly believe it.

I think many times we say we believe and don't really mean it, because if we did we wouldn't do half the things we do. Think about it. If we believe, we know the Lord is always with us, always. Keeping that fact in mind, we will try a little experiment. Lets say the Lord was standing next to you, right in the flesh. I mean you can see Him and He is right there in front of you. We will also say, He was there for the past twenty-four hours. Would you have acted the same as you did in that past twenty-four-hour period? Would you have done exactly the same things you did? My guess is your answer would be a big fat no! If it is a no, maybe you had better start re-evaluating what you do.

Oh yes, it is so easy to say I believe. It is so easy to say I love you, at least for many it seems. Do you really mean it? Words can be and often are cheap. We tend to throw out I love you's and I believe's like water, with no thought behind them, no genuine feelings to speak of, no sincerity involved, just nice words to say at the time.

If you truly believe, act like it! Prove it! Your actions make the statement! Please understand, I certainly do not mean to infer "all" words are cheap and without meaning. As an example, the Holy Bible would represent words of

- - - - - - - - - - - - - -

quite the opposite in nature and totally full of meaning, heartfelt, authentic or pure.

When you speak to your children, you need to teach them discernment. This could be one of your most formidable tasks. Your children need to be able to distinguish right from wrong. I know it sounds easy enough, but we don't give it the attention it deserves. Not everything is black and white, there are plenty of gray areas and this can be where the most problems lie.

We need to teach our children to be wary of people who say one thing, but their actions tell us something different. I find this especially true in politics and most probably the reason we are in the predicament we are in today. Politicians have made an art out of saying exactly what you would like them to say and achieving nothing short of stardom, only to find out later their actions tell us things completely different and many times the opposite of what they were preaching. I found to some degree the younger fall prey to this to the greatest extent, but the older more mature or seasoned are not exempt. Actually, I feel all ages can use help in this area.

Maybe some more communications at the dinner table could help us all. This is exactly why I say we need to get back to the basics. When we go back to the basics, a lot of things become eminently more clear. Not only do things become more obvious, but going back to the basics gives us a gauge to use to measure the credibility of others, their actions and their words. When we teach our children these things, it also helps us to reinforce the basics in our own minds, which tend to accumulate dust and cobwebs themselves.

We Need a Dinner Table!

As an ex-college professor, I have found one of the best ways to learn something or reinforce something in my mind was to teach it. What I'm trying to say here is that while teaching your children you are not only helping them, but yourself. You are reminding yourselves of the basics, while making them known to your children. Sometimes while doing this you might find areas where you, yourself may be lacking and need help in. You see, as a teacher or a professor you are the one who is supposed to have all the answers. This is how the student thinks anyway. It may be hard to believe and this is just an estimate, but I would say approximately eighty-five per cent of what I taught, I was never taught myself. The last statement might surprise you, but I know many others who could say the same.

As a pedagogue of your children you might find yourself in some very precarious situations. If you know you are going to have a discussion with your children on a certain subject you should, at the very least, go over the discussion in your mind and prepare answers to questions on the material you think they probably will or might ask. I tell you this for the sake of preventing you from getting you caught up in an embarrassing moment. You will quickly find that ad-libbing the conversation doesn't always work, in fact many times can get you into quite a mess. Be prepared, is the best way to express it. Even for the simplest of topics a little preparation can go a long way.

When you speak to your children don't, be making things up as you go along. They may be young and naive, but they are smarter than you think and they will be able to tell. Don't underestimate the intelligence of your children! I don't know, maybe by instinct or something, but they will know and it could be embarrassing. This is why I say to make sure you review these things beforehand in your mind.

I know you have all been to school before and you know when the professor is prepared and when he or she isn't, even when you don't know of the material from which they teach. It's usually pretty obvious and a situation you would not care to be in. Been there, done that and worked very hard never to be caught again.

Another thing I found out while teaching is to always start at square one. I need to emphasize this especially when teaching the basics! I know I have already said not to underestimate your child's intelligence, but at the same time, when teaching, assume they know nothing. I know that may sound contradictory, but I will explain.

If I were to start explaining something to my child and said to them, "When should you obey the fourth commandment?" Your child answers "Always." Sounds like a good answer to me and it is. Enough said, right? Well, not necessarily. What if you were to come back later and ask of your child, "What is the fourth commandment anyway?" Your child's reply, the same child, "I don't know." Hmm, I guess that means there is more work that needs to be done. What you should see here is we are assuming the child knew what the fourth commandment was right from the beginning and we assumed wrong. A better way would have been to first ask the child what the fourth commandment is and then to ask them when they should obey it.

We Need a Dinner Table!

You should also be prodding your children to find out exactly how much they really do know. You may ask something like what is so good about the Holy Bible, you just may be surprised at their answer. Maybe asking something like which God do they believe in. You could also ask how long are people suppose to be married or when should they get divorced. Its okay to lie if it is just a "white" lie right? You know, those trick questions. How about saying, "It's okay to steal from someone as long as they stole something from you first before right?" Asking very general type questions can reveal a lot about how they perceive things, their interpretations and their basic understanding of very important issues.

Your child's entire childhood should be one long, never ending learning experience. How can you make this happen? A very good starting place is at the old dinner table, not the only place, but a good starting place. Prod them there and find out what they do know and what they don't. If you find they are really lacking in a certain area set some time aside, to help them, instruct them and give them what they need to go out into the world with. The dinner table is also a great place to inform your children on you, who you are, your childhood experiences, what your parents, their grandparents, were like when you were their age. I use to love hearing my father's stories of his past experiences. I could have listened to them all day and night.

Don't neglect to tell your children about their ancestors and their family history. It shocks me on how little teenagers know about their own families and their families history. What do you talk to your children about? Maybe

We Need a Dinner Table!

– – – – – – – – – – –

I should ask, "Do you talk to your children at all?" I know many of you do these things already, but I also know there are many who do not and are the ones we need to help. Your children don't learn these things by chance or mistake. It's your duty as parents to prepare your children for the world and beyond.

Teaching your children doesn't have to be a bad, boring or mean kind of thing. Make it fun and interesting. Clue them in on some of your funny and interesting experiences, everyone has them. Let them know your most embarrassing moment, it might have been embarrassing then, but really funny now. It will show them your human side and what you did to cope with your own problems or embarrassing situations and how the world didn't come to an end, because of it. This is teaching too! They might very well run into some very similar experiences and remember how you handled it. If you handled the experience improperly, tell them, let them know, they will see that too and learn not to do the same. You can tell them what you should have done, but didn't and they'll learn from it. These are all learning experiences and invaluable to your children. They will appreciate your candor and respect you for it, not think less of you.

What I have been doing is describing how my parents handled me and how even today I love them for it and wouldn't trade it for a world of riches. Their ways, although not perfect, helped me immensely in getting me through some of the worst times and where I stand today. I consider the privilege of having my particular parents a priceless gift from the Lord Himself. A treasure you can't measure in terms of money.

- - - - - - - - - - - - - -

We Need a Dinner Table!

I think you would like your children to feel the same way about you as I feel for my parents. You need to talk to your children, communicate with them and they will love you for it. Much of what I learned began right at the dinner table. Notice I said "began", it might be where it begins, but once begun, it really never ends, even after they leave home and go on their own.

I will leave you with one last thing you may communicate to your children, with some wisdom taught by my father to me. He said, "Befriend everyone, make everyone your friend, because if everyone is your friend it will leave you with no enemies." Amen .....

Chapter 9

We Are Roman Catholics!

Let it be known! We have been silent long enough. We do have freedom of speech in this country. Yes, it does apply to Christians too, even to Roman Catholics, even though sometimes you may get the impression we are the only ones it doesn't apply to. We are over seventy million strong, according to a 2008 survey, so let it be known!

I get the feeling there is a small faction in the United States who have a vendetta against Christians in general. They come nowhere near our numbers, but they are loud in voice and are constantly trying to get any kind of Christian religion stripped from being displayed or heard anywhere in the United States through our court systems. They have been somewhat successful, because many times those with the loudest mouth's wins.

They are no where near the majority, but often they gain control of the majority, because they are not shy in letting their presence known. We need to go to combat against these people or it will get worse. We need to get loud and stand up for our rights and freedoms!

I know the mind set for many Christians and especially Roman Catholics are to be meek, gentle, patient, passive and to walk in humility. Normally I wouldn't have a problem with that as I, for the most part, act quite the same. However, there comes a time where you need to stand up and say enough is enough and get up and fight for your rights before they get taken away one by one.

We can get as loud as they are and get much louder if we want to. We have the numbers to drown out those who want to take our religious freedoms away easily. We can't do it buy being silent, we have to take action. We need to speak out and if necessary fight them in the courts. If their small numbers can do it, we would have no problem with the numbers behind us.

We need to do this not only for ourselves, but for our children and their children. If we expect our children to have the same freedoms in religion as we do, we are going to have to work to do it. I don't think you want your children to go to school and end up getting expelled for saying the name Jesus or drawing a picture in art class of a cross. Guess what? It has happened already, in both instances.

This nonsense needs to be stopped! You can't even sing Christmas carols in some schools! Our children do this for years and now all of a sudden its reason for suspension? How far are we going to let this go? Are we waiting until they take every last freedom we have? Soon there will only be one place where we will be able to freely speak our religion. It will be in a cave somewhere and maybe while we are there we can display a crucifix if we keep watch at the entrance of the cave. Is this what we want? Does this need to happen before we do anything?

I happen to be as much of a peace-loving person as the next person, but where are we going to draw the line? Aren't you getting as sick of this as I happen to be? I thought we were in trouble years ago already, but I know we are now. I have no doubt in my mind. They are closing in on us real fast and I see very few of us doing anything about it. We can do it, we have the numbers! What are we waiting for?

This books main objectives are to get Crusade #1 going and to help save the unborn babies in this nation and the world. It's at the top of the list, because we are talking the loss of millions of lives and needs to be put to rest yesterday! There is a long "list" of things, however, that we should be working together on. If we don't even fight for our children rights in the schools, how are we ever going to reverse the abortion laws?

I see nothing. Nothing is happening. Why isn't there anything happening? This is what I ask myself all of the time. I happen to be guilty too, but I couldn't take it anymore. This kind of thing would never have happened years ago. Our ancestors were fighters and now I understand why. If you don't fight to keep your freedoms there will always be someone there to try and take them away. We have been really lucky, we have enjoyed our religious freedoms for quite a long time now, with the main exception being that of abortion, which is a big exception and a very sick one.

We Are Roman Catholics!

Besides abortion another objective of this book is to stir up the masses of our members in the Roman Catholic community here in the United States. We need to get going. We need to get the ball rolling and straighten out the wrongs pitted against us. I don't want to be an embarrassed to be a Roman Catholic. I love our religion. I use to be a real fighter, when I was younger, but in aging I have grown very passive. I can change if need be to protect the freedoms of our religion, can you? It is going to take change. We can't keep going on as we are now.

You had to have noticed how bad things are getting or you must already be in that cave with your crucifix I was talking about before. It doesn't take a person with eagle eyes to see all the things we have to correct right now. Who knows what is coming next? Every day there is some other right we have, which is being taken away and yet I see no one doing anything. Shame on you, shame on me!

We don't have to live with this or live like this. We need to take up where our ancestors left off and fight to maintain our religious freedoms. We already have most of our freedoms, we just need to fight to keep them. There are some freedoms we need to get back and some laws we need to change, so we do have our work cut out.

Personally, what I would really like is not to have to worry about any of these things. I would like to be able to talk about our religion anywhere I choose, within reason, of course. I would like to be able to go to a Christmas show put on by the kids at the elementary school without worrying about it being canceled due to political correctness. I would like to read in the paper about the local college team saying a prayer before the game and not getting in trouble because of it. I would like to hear they are returning the Ten Commandment displays in front of all of our courthouses. I would like to hear they are re-instituting the prayer in the morning at all the public schools for those who would like to participate. I would like to hear that an art student at school painted a beautiful crucifix and didn't get into trouble. Above all, I would love to hear on the national news, that our abortion laws have just been overturned by the supreme court, so it is now illegal to have an abortion and there is no longer any need to have this book! This is what I would really, really like to hear and see.

It could happen, but only if we get together on this and make it happen. If nothing changes, if nothing happens, I can only assume my brothers and sisters in the Roman Catholic faith don't care. If it is true, I guess I have a right to be ashamed and embarrassed of the members of our religion. I hope your faith is better than that. No matter what, I will never be ashamed of our religion, maybe our members, but never our religion, because I know our religion tells us what our duties are and what it takes to be a good Christian. If we don't do our duties, then I guess we deserve what we get.

I see a great need for many of our Church members to purchase a catechism book almost as much as the need for a Holy Bible. If you haven't seen a Roman Catholic catechism book, you should. There is plenty of good information on the proper way a good and practicing Roman Catholic should act both morally and spiritually, what your duties is, the Ten Commandments, the Church precepts, the sacraments, the Church itself, what we believe in and why and I can go on and on and on. If you need a refresher course in the Roman Catholic religion, you need to get this book. It also makes a great reference book when situations arise and you are unsure on how to handle them.

If you have strayed from our religion, it is time to get back. We need all the help we can get. If you don't like the immorality and corruption going on here in these great United States come back to our religion, talk to a priest or nun and ask them what you can do to help. I know they will greet you with open arms and give you some direction so you too can help to get things back on the right path again. You can join the crusade, Crusade #1, for the abolition of abortion in the United States and the world. Later I will tell you how you can join the crusade and start saving the lives of unborn defenseless babies. I myself can't imagine how great it must feel to save one of these unborn babies from the fate of abortion, but it must feel like a little bit of heaven on earth as I see it. I would give all the credit to our Lord, but it would be nice simply to be the conduit from which the Lord does his great deeds. Remember you can't do anything without the Lord and anything you get comes from the Lord, so always be thankful and show your gratitude.

I have been getting off the track somewhat, but for good reason. All I'm really trying to say is that we should not be afraid to profess our faith in public, there is nothing to be ashamed of, afraid of or concerned about. We have a beautiful religion and we are all striving to have the best of virtues, to walk in humility, to act with morality and to love our brothers and sisters. If anyone has a problem with that, it's their problem, not yours. Just make sure you don't force yourself on anyone, believe it or not, if you handle it right, there are plenty of people willing to listen. I know I have tried.

I'm always trying to spread our faith. I haven't always been successful, but I keep on trying. I found I have the most luck with those who have no religion to speak of or have big misconceptions on exactly what we do believe in. I think I have good luck with those without religion, because they have no idea what they are missing and when they find out, it stirs up their curiosity and they start to ask questions. They start thinking and with some more work you might even get them to look into becoming a member of our religion. There are people out there, many of them, that just need to get clued in, because no one has ever seriously suggested religion to them in the first place. Why, I don't know, but quite unfortunate.

People around you do get accustomed to you speaking religion if you do it regularly. When I first mentioned religion at work, everyone cringed and wanted to hide. It was almost like I committed some kind of crime. I never realized how political correctness had taken such an effect on people. Ha, but that didn't stop me! I told them the truth and the truth is that we have freedom of speech in the United States and there is no law saying we can't talk about religion in public, at least not yet!. I also made it a point to mention something about our religion every day in my work place and now my fellow employees have become use to it and bring it up themselves at times. We have some very interesting discussions and I know I have been arousing their interest and teaching them its ok to speak religion and maybe even a good thing. I also have been educating them in what they thought was a Roman Catholic to whom really a Roman Catholic is. Most often there are big misconceptions. They are finding out what we believe isn't really all that bad and they believe pretty much the same things or at least open to our beliefs.

This is why I say we need to step out and let our faith be known after all it is our duty. Once you break the ice a bit you will find many people who are receptive and interested in what you have to say. I would recommend you take it slow and don't try to cover too much too fast. Let what you have to say, sink in for a while and don't give them so much at once that they get lost or confused. I think you will be surprised how much they want to know and learn if you try it.

Many of the people I speak to feel the same way on most of the moral issues and about the corruption they see. Many of them would like to see the same changes we should be seeking in our government and our laws. Check it out for yourselves. It's what I have found and it's my guess you will find it too.

Let the people know we are Roman Catholics and we really aren't that bad at all. Spread the word, let it be known, shout it out if you have to, clear up all the misconceptions. It's our right, it's our duty and it will make you feel good knowing you are doing the right thing. You are doing the right thing not only for yourself, but for your brothers and sisters. Prove your love of your neighbor by trying to get them all in heaven!

Chapter 10

Be Prudent and Vigilant!

O pen your eyes and ears, be prudent and vigilant. I think this is yet another big problem we have. We need to have some common sense and we need to be very watchful. Evil is alive and well in the United States. If you don't already know that or realize that you need to wake up. If you go through life with your eyes closed, when you finally decide to open them you may find a big surprise. Not a good surprise, but a big one, an evil one.

I don't know if we are hiding from it, ignoring it or living in some kind of dream world. In any case, it is not good and we need to become more vigilant, more alert and increasingly aware of the evil in our country, our states and our cities. You can't act on evil, stop evil or prevent evil if you're not even cognizant of the fact it exists! You might ask, "Well, what do I do?" It may not be your fault

- - - - - - - - - - - - - -

entirely, but your fault or not, you need to correct it and what you have to do is, first of all, recognize it exists.

I know many people who do not keep up with, current events, stay away from the news and avoid politics like the plague. Normally I would say, if that is the way you are, it's not necessarily a bad thing. I would say, in the world today, it isn't a very prudent way to be. I wouldn't say it is bad, but common sense should tell us we need to be more aware of what is going on around us, especially in these times.

I wouldn't say you need to participate in these activities twenty-four hours a day, seven days a week. I think we do need to, at a minimum, be aware of current events, both on a local and a national level. Checking out the major headlines and events don't take long and will help to make you aware of important happenings, which may affect our religion, both of a good and bad nature.

In politics, you need to participate by voting and knowing what you are voting for. This means knowledge of the candidates and their platforms. This may take a little more time than the news, but not that much more time. If you are to help out our religion and expect to maintain your religious rights and freedoms it would be prudent to gain as much knowledge as possible for exercising good judgement when choosing your candidate and placing your vote.

It is necessary, but not as tough as it might sound to find out the important information needed to place a quality vote for the Church, our religion and for you at the same time. If you, like most of us, have internet access, you can find these things out rather quickly by going straight to the candidates web sites. Many times while looking over the major headlines, you can find out the major points in a candidate's platform.

I hope we know voting on a candidate, because he or she is good looking or you just like their name is not an acceptable reason for placing something so important as your vote. You only get one vote, don't waste it! It could be years before you get another chance to vote and a politician could do a lot of damage to our religious rights and freedoms in the meantime.

In order to be prudent and vigilant and protect your religion you need to be cognizant, recognize and be aware of what is going on around you and in our country. It takes a little extra time, but can be extremely important to you, your children and your faith. Ideally you shouldn't have to worry about it as far as I'm concerned, but how many things in our world are ideal? With that question in mind it is best to do the extra work and rest easy knowing you are doing it for the good of everyone.

It is really a small price to pay when you think about it. Our men in uniform, the men in our armed forces have many times given their lives, so all we have to worry about is placing a good vote to maintain our freedoms and preserve justice for all in our land.

We also need to be aware of the politician. I say this, because the politician many times will say anything and everything to get your vote. You listen to these politicians and they sound really very good. You like everything they say. Later, once elected, you find those same politicians do exactly the opposite of what they have preached. This is not good, but it happens all the time and you have to be wary of it.

When it comes to politicians, you need to pay more attention to their actions, then their words. You need to listen to them, but you also need to see if they follow through with what they have preached to you to get your vote. This tends to be the most important thing to watch for, because who cares what they say if they do the opposite?

Some politicians are quite slick and will do and say what is necessary to get elected, whether they intend to follow through or not. I feel some of the best things to know about a politician is their past history of voting, their moral conduct and behavior. If the candidate appears to have little or no morals do you want to trust your vote to him or her? I have seen a politician be convicted of a felony, more than once, get re-elected to office right here in the state of Pennsylvania when he got out of prison! Do you think this is a wise move? Sound hard to believe doesn't it? Maybe so, but true! Sometimes fact is stranger than fiction. I know that politician wouldn't be getting my vote. For the life of me I can't understand how something like that could possibly happen.

These are the things we have to deal with, out there. We are over seventy million strong and we can do it as a team working together with each other. It is necessary we work together and necessary we are all on the same page for us to be effective.

I just recently heard on a radio broadcast a very smug person speaking about the abortion laws in an interview. He was saying how abortions are now the law of the land, so just live with it and move on. Oh how sweet is he! It's the law of the land, so that is it. I wanted to, well I can't say what I wanted to do, but I counted to ten to allow the steam to clear from my ears. How can a person have such a little regard for our tiny unborn babies lives? Such disrespect for the sanctity of life? Is this how we want our society to think and act? Personally, I think it is so disgusting, I want to puke. Sorry for the graphics, but it is so true!

I don't want a country with people thinking and acting in this manner. I really hope you feel the same way. Abortion may truly be the law of the land right now, but I sincerely believe it can be changed if we organize our efforts against it. We will not change it by being silent and laying down and rolling over! We will need to organize and fight or accept it. I'm not ready to accept it at all and never will be ready to accept it. I can't believe my fellow brothers and sisters in the Roman Catholic faith can accept this either.

Prudence, common sense and vigilance, being wary of what is going on, are part of the fight against this evil, but only part of the fight. It is a very important part of the puzzle necessary to combat these evil laws. Crossing the street is easy, but if you cross the street without looking and listening it could end in a catastrophe.

To sum things up, we need to understand how important it is to be watchful of the events going on around us. We need to use a little common sense and realize the need for all of us to work together. These things will be our tools to use to fight the corruption and bad laws that exist already in this great nation.

I know my path keeps following the trails of abortion

— — — — — — — — — —

and the abortion laws. Abortion is on my mind always. I keep thinking what if I were one of those unborn babies? It hurts me so much to hear the callous remarks of so many people in this country who don't even give abortion a second thought. I can't understand how people can be so emotionally hardened and unfeeling. I would say I hope I never become that way, but I know there is no chance whatsoever of that ever happening with me. I just want to make sure it doesn't happen to anyone else, because if it does we are lost and this won't be the great United States I remember anymore.

It's a scarey and sad thought, that if we just live our lives, Christian lives, and do no harm to no one, we still have the worry of evil taking over our society. It shouldn't be that way, but the sad fact is that it is. This being the fact, makes prudence and vigilance most important in our lives. This way we can prepare to fight it, otherwise we won't even see it coming and by the time we do it will be too late.

We have a lot of people depending on us. We have our families, our relatives, our friends and all our brothers and sisters expecting to live with justice and our freedoms in our country. We can't disappoint them! We need to get this country back under control and in the right hands of honest and morally upright individuals so as to preserve the riches of this wonderful country.

It is not going to be an easy fight, because things are way out of control already. When we don't care if our unborn babies, live or die, we have big problems! I firmly believe the task isn't impossible if we work together hand-in-hand.

- - - - - - - - - - - -

Be Prudent and Vigilant!
— — — — — — — — — — —

I think we all want our country to be rich in spirituality, morals and respect. What great resources for a country to have, worth working and fighting for. Don't you think?

Part III
The Finale

Chapter 11

Anything Else!

I did it! I spilled out all of my guts to you, everything. I had to get everything off my chest and to let you know my feelings on a lot of things, especially abortion. You know me better than my family does now. These are most of the things I hold nearest and dearest to my heart.

If I hurt anyone's feelings, I apologize, it wasn't my intent. Sometimes you have to be a bit bold to emphasize the importance of a point. My only goal is to, with your help, save the lives of the defenseless unborn babies in danger of being aborted and to get us Roman Catholic back on the track of truth and righteousness or the path of light.

I thought I was raised pretty good and had an advantage over many people because of it. Besides the abortion issue, I have tried to outline what I believe is a good way to raise children and to act towards others. You may not agree with everything I have said, but I thought you might value some of my experiences. I sincerely hope you can find some good in what I have said and can put it to good use.

I would like you to do a big favor for me. If you haven't noticed, but up until now, when speaking about abortion, I have not used the terms' fetus, embryo, organism or any other terms of the like. I would like you to do the same. When referring to an unborn baby, call it that, an unborn baby, please! I believe when we use the other terms we forget we are talking about an unborn baby and now abortion, all of a sudden, doesn't sound so bad. We need to "always" remember we are talking about a baby, no matter if it is before birth or after. Thank you in advance!

I also have three recommendations for you before I retire. First, pray, pray, pray, pray and pray some more for all the unborn babies of the world. Pray that they will not succumb to the fate of abortion. Please make it one of your daily prayers. I personally know prayer works and the more we have praying, the better.

Second, "live" your faith! Don't be all talk and no action. Participate in Crusade #1, don't just sit there. There are unborn babies dying every minute of every day. If you see, wrongs against the Lord's laws do something about it. Make your vote count, vote for people who respect the sanctity of life, the Lord's Ten Commandments and the constitution, which gives us our religious rights and freedoms. Get organized at your Church with your relatives, friends and others. We could do anything if we do it together and right all the wrongs we already have in our society.

Anything Else!

— — — — — — — — — — — —

Finally, be strong! Don't be afraid to defend you rights as a Christian and a Roman Catholic. Remember, we have God on our side. With God on our side we can end up with a really wonderful country and really mean it when we say, **"One Nation, Under God"** and say, "Yes, I do have the nerve to call myself a Roman Catholic!" Amen .....

Chapter 12

About the Author.

Right about now, you are probably wondering who is this guy anyway? I don't blame you and I would probably say the same.

I would like to take this time to thank you for your purchase of this book. Please see to it that anyone contemplating abortion gets a copy. Hopefully, working together, we can eliminate this abomination from the face of the earth.

It's nothing spectacular, but I will give you a brief rundown of my life, so you will have an idea of whom you have been dealing with.

I was born in Northampton, Pennsylvania, USA in 1954. I was born a "U.S. Navy Brat", that would be the son of a father enlisted in the U.S. Navy. This is important to know, because being a "Navy Brat" means you move when your parents move and if your father is in the U.S.

- - - - - - - - - - - - - - -

About the Author.

Navy it means you move approximately every two years, because in my father's position it is a typical requirement to be transferred to different duty stations in that time period. This means I have lived in several locations throughout my life, such as: Pennsylvania, New Jersey, Florida, California, Rhode Island and South Carolina. I may have missed a place or two, but I think you get the idea. Once I reached the seventh grade I moved back to Pennsylvania and stayed until I graduated high school.

I graduated Northampton Area Senior High School in 1972.

Upon graduating high school I entered the U.S. Navy myself as a signalman and completed one tour of duty obtaining my highest rank of E-5 or petty officer second class. I served most of my duty on the U. S. Navy destroyer U.S.S. Aylwin, which is now called a fast frigate.

During my stay in the U.S. Navy I completed three Mediterranean cruises, one Mideast cruise, One cruise up the Hudson River and several Carribean or Gitmo (Guantanamo Bay, Cuba) cruises for war training. I was discharged in 1975 at my home base in Norfolk, Virginia.

After leaving the U.S. Navy I decided to stay in Norfolk, Virginia and attended Old Dominion University. I entered the university as a matriculated electrical engineering student.

In 1980 I moved back to Pennsylvania and held several jobs in the electronics field:

Building, testing and converting analogue gauges to digital gauges in the R & D shop for a division of the Ford

_ _ _ _ _ _ _ _ _ _ _ _

Motor Company.

Electrical communications for installing mobile telephones in vehicles and repairing and troubleshooting communication antennas.

A production troubleshooter of digital computer peripherals for the space shuttle, NASA, U.S. Navy jet electronic nose cones and electronic equipment for the general public.

During this same time period I was also married and had two beautiful daughters, Deborah and Melissa.

In 1983 I became certified in Pennsylvania as a college professor teaching:

- Basic Electronics
- Advanced Electronics
- Mathematics
- Physics
- Programming
- AM/FM Radio
- TV Electronics
- Electronic Communications
- Speed Reading

In 1989 I moved to Florida, became certified in California and Florida to teach, continuing as a college professor at the U.S. Naval base in Orlando. There I taught:

About the Author.

- Basic Electronics
- Advanced Electronics
- Electronics Safety
- Mathematics
- Communications
- CB Radio
- Antennas
- Waveguides

This should give you somewhat of an idea of my background and some of the highlights of my life. The Lord was very good to me and allowed three of my childhood wishes. One, to become a sailor in the U.S. Navy and see the world. Two, to become versed in the field of electronics and computers. Three, to become a mathematics professor.

I now reside in Pennsylvania where I have been for the past fifteen years, approximately. My daughters have grown into two beautiful young ladies a father could be very proud of and is. I haven't accomplished all my goals in life, but many of them, thank you Lord. Finally, my latest and one of my most important goals, is to get our nation back on track in the elimination of abortion, but not only here, also in the world. Wish me luck, please .....

Part IV
- Bonus -
Special Reader's
Challenge!

Chapter 13

Surprise Challenge!

Lucky chapter thirteen. I hope you didn't read this chapter first! Yes, I do have a surprise for you and a challenge for you! I intend to write a sequel to this book, but with your help. I need your interaction to make it happen.

When the sequel is completed this book and the next, from that point on will be offered as a two-book set. There are 224 pages in this book and what I would like to do is to have a minimum of 224 pictures of "saved" babies pictured in it, who were in danger of being aborted, but were "saved". I will use the number of pages in this book to set the arbitrary minimum for the next.

I would like you to help me get those "saved" babies. I need you to do this, when you hear of or find out about any couples or anyone considering abortion. Give them a copy of this book, then sit down with them and convince

- - - - - - - - - - - - - - -

them abortion is never an option. Let them have a copy of the book, so they can read it and let everything sink in. Talk to them some more and guide them down the righteous path, the path of light. Hopefully you can convince them to have their baby and a baby will be "saved".

When you do this, I want to know about it. In fact, if in any way possible you can save a baby from the fate of abortion I want to know about it. You know, whatever works!

Next, I would like you to send me a short explanation on how you helped save the baby. After the baby is born and before the baby is three months old, send me a picture of the baby and the mother or just the baby will do. The picture and short explanation will go into the sequel of this book.

It will take some time, but with your help we can get enough "saved" babies for every page of this book. Those who purchase the two-book set thereafter will have a book to help explain why abortion is wrong and also have a book showing them the results of pro-life, the beautiful babies who have been "saved", either due to this book or simply due to our efforts.

It is my guess, that the second book, would make a wonderful clincher in convincing couples abortion is just flat out wrong! How could anyone look at all those beautiful "saved" babies in the sequel and not be convinced? In this way you could be part of the crusade, Crusade #1, to abolish abortion, but most of all you will have saved the life of an unborn baby!

The Challenge! I will be working on saving babies

myself. I will try to get as many pictures in the second book as I can, see if you can top me! My challenge to you is to get more pictures of saved babies than me. I can't do this without help, your help, please. Working together, we can fill that second book up in no time.

I know your next question, "How do I send you my information and pictures?" RDR Publishing LLC, the publisher of this book, has graciously developed a web site which is dedicated specifically for this purpose. They will also be publishing the pictures you send to the web site, so internet surfers can view them, at least until the sequel of this book is ready for publishing. We just might get some converts that way too! The web site is open to anyone and everyone to try to get converts there also. The more avenues we pursue, the more chances we will have to save an unborn baby. This is our goal and the more unborn babies saved the better! The web site address is:

Web Site:
www.RDRPublishing.com
E-Mail:
info@RDRPublishing.com

When you get your information together along with the picture go to the web site, "Contact Us", page. There you will see a short form to fill out and a drop down menu for the message heading with a choice on it saying "One More Saved!" This is where you can enter your information and e-mail your picture. You can also use the publisher's, RDR Publishing, mailing address to send your information and pictures by snail mail if you prefer at:

Surprise Challenge!

— — — — — — — — — — —

RDR Publishing LLC
P. O. Box 441
Bethlehem, Pa. 18016-0441

Either way I will be sitting on the edge of my seat waiting to hear from you. I can't wait to read your stories and to see your successes! Every picture I get will make my day and put a smile on my face from ear-to-ear! This can be our own personal crusade and challenge.

See if you can beat the challenge! I will be working on saving babies, so you will have your work cut out. I'm not going to make it easy for you. My goal is at least ten converts or "saved" babies. Keywords here are "at least", if I can get more you can bet I will. As soon as the minimum is reached, I will put the sequel together to make up the two-book set. Who knows, if we could get enough together, I will make it a three-book set! That would be 448 "saved" babies! Wow! I would be in heaven on earth! With your help it can be done. I can't do it by myself, I need you. Let this book be a catalyst for better things to come. Take the challenge and save a baby.

When you go to the web site and visit our "Contact Us" page you will have some other opportunities to utilize. Besides using the "One More Saved!", option you will be given other options. You may use any or all of the options if you so desire to.

You will have the "Book Critique" option. This should be fairly self-explanatory. Here you can let us know of any

- - - - - - - - - - - - - -

changes, improvements you would care to see/offer or any additions you would like to see done to the book itself. We are graciously open to any suggestions you might have.

You will have the "My Plan- The Vote", option. In this book we made suggestions for the crusade, "Crusade #1", pertaining to voting. Here is your chance. Do you have a better idea? If you do, let us know! We would be very happy to hear your thoughts and ideas.

Next, you will have the "Join The Crusade", option. Get on our mailing list and join our crusade, Crusade #1, for the abolition of abortion in the United States of America and the world! Become a member and as we get and develop more information we will keep you posted. We will send you details of any events and any other information and ideas that come our way.

Finally, you will have the "Other", option. This option is for anything we may have left out. Got some constructive criticism? Let us know. This is for any and all things you might have on your mind about the abortion issue or any issues you may be concerned with and would like to share with us.

Well, there you have it. Now it is time to get to work and save our unborn babies from the fate of abortion. Meet and beat the challenge! Please help these unborn babies, they are defenseless without you, they need you. Do it for the glory of God ..... Amen .....

Bibliography

The American Heritage Dictionary. Vers. 3.6p. InfoSoft International, Inc., 1980. Computer Software.

Attwater, Donald, ed. *A Catholic Dictionary*. Third ed. Rockford: Tan Books And Publishers, Inc., 1997. Print.

Catechism of the Catholic Church. Second ed. Washington: United States Catholic Conference, 2000. Print.

Holy Bible (New American Bible). The Catholic Bible Giant Print ed. Witchita: DeVore and Sons, Inc., 1981. Print.

- - - - - - - - - - - - - - -